# DROPPIN' KNOWLEDGE ON PHONICS

Heidi Martin

Adam Martin

# DROPPIN' KNOWLEDGE ON PHONICS

Spelling and Phonics Activities Aligned to the Science of Reading

**JB JOSSEY-BASS™**

A Wiley Brand

Published by John Wiley & Sons, Inc., Hoboken, New Jersey.
Published simultaneously in Canada.

ISBNs: 9781394261505 (Paperback), 9781394261512 (ePub), 9781394261529 (ePDF)

For general information on our other products and services, please contact our Customer Care Department within the United States at (800) 762-2974, outside the United States at (317) 572-3993. For product technical support, you can find answers to frequently asked questions or reach us via live chat at https://support.wiley.com/s/.

If you believe you've found a mistake in this book, please bring it to our attention by emailing our reader support team at wileysupport@wiley.com with the subject line "Possible Book Errata Submission."

Wiley also publishes its books in a variety of electronic formats. Some content that appears in print may not be available in electronic formats. For more information about Wiley products, visit our website at www.wiley.com.

*Library of Congress Control Number:* 2025001207 (print)

Cover Design and Images: Wiley

SKY10100184_031525

# Contents

## Wrapping Up

# About the Authors

**Heidi Martin** is trained in LETRS for Early Childhood, IMSE Orton-Gillingham, and Top 10 Tools. She is a National Facilitator for LETRS EC. She has presented at national conferences as well as provided training at the district level. Heidi is the author of *P is for Paint*, which is the one and only alphabet book with embedded mnemonics. She has authored and self-published the Decodable Adventure Series books. She taught first grade for over 10 years and most recently taught Kindergarten and 4K.

**Adam Martin** is a National LETRS Facilitator certified Units 1–8 and presents to teachers and districts on a weekly basis. He has his Masters in Educational Literacy and his Reading Specialist License. He is the co-author and editor for the Decodable Adventure Series. He taught first grade for seven years and has tutored children of all ages.

## How to Contact the Authors

We appreciate your input and questions about this book! Email us at hello@droppinknowledge.com or visit our website at www.droppinknowledge.com.

## Other Books in the *Droppin' Knowledge* Series

*Droppin' Knowledge on Sight Words and Word Mapping: High-Frequency Word Activities Aligned to the Science of Reading*

*Droppin' Knowledge on Foundational Skills: Phonological and Phonemic Awareness Activities Aligned to the Science of Reading*

# Hey, Parents and Teachers!

We are so excited to help you teach reading! We are Heidi and Adam Martin—both former first-grade teachers (and parents) who now spend our time sharing the Science of Reading with as many people as we can! But before this, we **had no idea there was a science to how we learn to read**. We taught first grade for a combined 15+ years using what most people call "balanced literacy" methods until we found that there is actual science to how we learn to read.

We also learned that according to the 2022 Nation's Report Card, less than 40% of kids are reading proficiently.[1] To us, this was a big wake-up call. If over 60% of our kids are not reading proficiently, we must be doing something wrong!

Once we learned there was decades of evidence and research on how we learn to read, we set out on a mission to unlearn and learn it all. We want to let you know that this has been a journey, not a sprint. There was a lot for us to unlearn (and still is). Throughout this journey of unlearning, we definitely had to work through some ups and downs, as well as emotions of frustration, anger, and regret. The fact that we were not taught this earlier, especially since this science has been around for over 20 years, can really weigh on you. We often think back to the kids we could have helped if we only knew what we know now. However, you don't know better until you do, so we just have to move forward and make sure this doesn't happen again. If some of this is new to you as well, please remember to give yourself grace!

Let's talk about some of the terms we have been using and clarify where we came from and where we are now.

# What Is Balanced Literacy?

Balanced literacy sounds good doesn't it? I mean who doesn't love being balanced? Heidi was sold on this, especially being a type B teacher. She was not a fan of words like "systematic" and "structured." Then, she found out that balanced literacy is not truly balanced after all. Adam was starting his teaching career being taught about the Science of Reading through his licensure program. However, in our school district, we were using balanced literacy curriculums. Going through hours of professional development on this curriculum, this became the norm. Since this was all the buzz, it had to be the most beneficial thing for our

---

[1]https://www.nationsreportcard.gov/reading/nation/achievement/?grade=4.

students, right? Adam said, "I had my skepticisms on balanced literacy, especially since I was seeing minimal progress from my students. I think this is the case for a lot of teachers."

To be clear, when we say balanced literacy, we are talking about programs and strategies that were most often used in schools and called "balanced" within those schools and programs. In reality, these programs skip many of the foundational reading skills kids need in order to become successful readers.

Balanced literacy was supposed to be the answer to the reading wars—a compromise. However, in our experience, there is much more of the whole language approach in balanced literacy programs. We feel that these "balanced literacy" programs are not truly balanced after all. Some examples of the remnants of whole language are:

- Skipping a word if you don't know it
- Using meaning or context to solve or read a word
- Believing that reading is natural (aka reading more will help kids become good readers)
- Memorizing "sight words" or spelling words

If our kids cannot decode and read the words on a page (or if they are skipping words), how will they "naturally" become skilled readers? We have learned from the research on how we learn to read that the continuum, or progression of learning to read, is NEVER truly balanced. We spend more time on specific skills when students are developing foundational reading skills than we do later on once those skills and abilities to decode are mastered. The time spent on specific skills will vary based on where our kids are in their reading development. So, although it sounds good, there is never really a "balance" to literacy.

# What Is the Science of Reading?

You have probably heard the term "Science of Reading" more times than you can count, but the definition can get a little muddy. So let's talk about what the Science of Reading is **not**.

The Science of Reading is not a curriculum.

The Science of Reading is not just phonics.

The Science of Reading is not a strategy or activity.

Here is how The Reading League defines the Science of Reading[2]:

The Science of Reading is a vast, interdisciplinary body of scientifically based research about reading and issues related to reading and writing. This research has been conducted over the last five decades across the world.

It is derived from thousands of studies conducted in multiple languages. The Science of Reading has culminated in a preponderance of evidence to inform how proficient reading and writing develop; why some have difficulty; and how we can most effectively assess and teach and, therefore, improve student outcomes through prevention of and intervention for reading difficulties.

The Science of Reading is derived from researchers from multiple fields:

Cognitive psychology

Communication sciences

Developmental psychology

Education

Implementation science

Linguistics

Neuroscience

School psychology

To break that down, we like to say that **the Science of Reading is the research and the evidence on how our brains learn to read**. This means that not just one study is referenced when discussing the skills kids need to read. Again, this is research that has been conducted for almost 50 years and includes research of the research (meta-analysis)!

We hope that helps explain some of the terms you may have been hearing about and why we decided to write these books. We are so excited for you to use these activities with your students and/or your own children.

_____

[2]https://www.thereadingleague.org/wp-content/uploads/2022/03/Science-of-Reading-eBook-2022.pdf.

Honestly, as teachers who were trained in balanced literacy, we did not think highly of phonics or decodable books. Heidi even stopped giving spelling tests after her first year of teaching. She was under the impression that these things would take away from the love of reading.

Adam felt that teaching phonics was a supplement, and getting kids in books was the thing to do. My curriculum pushed this, and we had numerous professional development sessions stating this, so I must be doing the right thing ... right? Well, I should have known better. Especially since much of this didn't line up with what I learned when I was getting my teaching license. I did make progress with students. They began memorizing more words and moving up in their leveled readers. But then I would check on them in second grade, and their teachers were stating that they were struggling and even beginning to go backwards, or stagnant, in their reading. Now I know why. I spent our time getting kids to memorize a set of words and did not teach them skills to decode and read new words.

Now that we know better, we both often think back to our students who were struggling to learn how to read and realize this is exactly what they needed. If we're being honest, even our "readers" should have been taught these skills. What happened to them when they got to third or fourth grade? Were they still able to read? Could they decode new, bigger words? When memorizing words and looking at the pictures are no longer options, what do our students do?

We now understand the importance of spelling and phonics and we will tell you from experience ... it does not take away from the love of reading! Kids are actually excited to practice, and when they apply these skills and decode new words, you can see so much confidence light up on their faces!

# Let's Talk About Phonics Patterns

Phonics just means teaching kids to connect the sounds they hear in words to the letter or letters that spell that sound. Phonics patterns should be taught systematically and explicitly. We should introduce skills in a sequential way while building on previously taught skills.

For example, if we are teaching short vowels in this order:

> Short A
>
> Short E
>
> Short I
>
> Short O
>
> Short U

Then we can use short A and short E words in our short I resources. This reinforces the skills we taught earlier and also gives kids practice with the new skills! We should not use Short U words in our Short I resources because kids have not learned that skill yet.

**It is important to note that there is no decided upon scope and sequence.** Meaning, there is no right or wrong order in which to teach phonics skills. Most scope and sequences are similar though as they tend to go from easier skills to more difficult skills.

Here is the phonics scope and sequence that we developed. We looked at many other scope and sequences and also used our experience teaching first grade to develop this. All of our resources strictly follow this scope and sequence.

# Phonics Scope & Sequence

| Skill Group | SKILL |
|---|---|
| Orange | Short A |
| Orange | Short E |
| Orange | Short I |
| Orange | Short O |
| Orange | Short U |
| Orange | Long Vowels |
| Blue | Digraph (th) |
| Blue | Digraph (sh) |
| Blue | Digraph (wh) |
| Blue | Digraph (ch) |
| Blue | Digraph (ng) |
| Blue | Floss Rule |
| Blue | Beginning S Blends |
| Blue | Beginning L Blends |
| Blue | Beginning R Blends |
| Blue | Ending Blend (nk) |
| Blue | Ending Digraph (ck) |
| ED Ending | |
| Yellow | S as /Z/ |
| Yellow | VCe |

| Skill Group | SKILL |
|---|---|
| Soft C & G | |
| Yellow | Vowel Team (ee) |
| Yellow | Vowel Team (ea) |
| Yellow | Vowel Team (ai) |
| Yellow | Vowel Team (ay) |
| Yellow | Vowel Team (oa) |
| Yellow | Vowel Team (ow) |
| Yellow | Vowel Team (igh) |
| Yellow | Vowel Team (UE) |
| Green | L-Controlled |
| Green | Closed Syllable Exceptions |
| Green | Bossy R (ar) |
| Green | Bossy R (or) |
| Green | Bossy R (er) *most common |
| Green | Bossy R (ir) (ur) |
| Pink | Tricky Y (as E) |
| Pink | Tricky Y (as I) |
| Pink | Vowel Digraph (oo) |
| Pink | Vowel Digraph (aw) (au) |
| Pink | Diphthong (ow) (ou) |
| Pink | Diphthong (oi) (oy) |
| Pink | Schwa |

@droppinknowledgewithheidi

After we teach students a phonics pattern, we can help them practice reading and spelling words that contain that phonics pattern.

# Let's Take a Look at the Reading Brain

Understanding the reading brain has been very impactful for us in our journey of following the Science of Reading. We think this is because when we're talking about what the brain is doing while we're reading, this is concrete evidence from the field of neuroscience. We feel that this evidence is enough to put the reading wars to rest. We know what parts of the brain we need to activate in order for our kids to read, and this gives us the information we need in order to teach reading!

Heidi developed this simplified version of the reading brain to make it easy to understand and also be able to share with your students.

# The **Simple** View of the Reading Brain

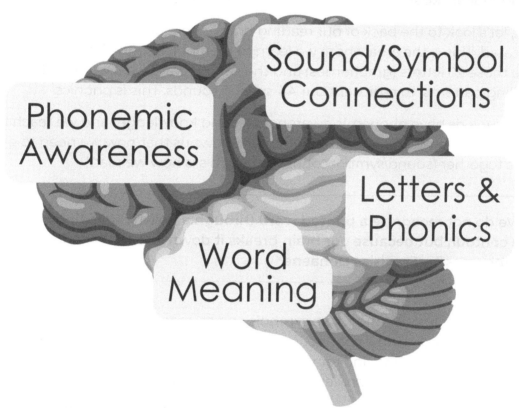

Sound/Symbol Connections

Phonemic Awareness

Letters & Phonics

Word Meaning

droppinknowledge.com

All of these parts must **work together** in order for us to read!

When we look at the Simple View of the Reading Brain, we want to first direct our attention to the front of the reading brain where our phonological processor is located. This is where phonemic awareness occurs, or where we manipulate language and sound. Research has taught us that before we can learn to read, we need to acquire oral language development. We also need an understanding of the 44 sounds (phonemes) we have in English, and the ability to manipulate those sounds. This is the bedrock, or foundation, to beginning to learn how to read (Speech to Print).

*For more information on this, check out our book* Droppin' Knowledge on Foundational Skills*!*

Next, let's look to the back of our reading brain where our orthographic processor is located. This is the area where we learn to manipulate print. This is where we store those 26 letters (graphemes) and the various ways we use those 26 letters (spelling patterns) to represent our 44 speech sounds. This is phonics!

Once our kids have phonemic awareness (sound knowledge) and we teach them letters and phonics skills, the reading brain shows us that now we need to put those together (sound/symbol connections). This is how we read!

> **"We do not recognize a printed word through a holistic grasping of its contour, but because our brain breaks it down into letters and graphemes." —Stanislas Dehaene**[3]

As our kids are connecting those symbols and sounds to decode, we can now look at the sound/symbol connection area of the brain. This is the area of the brain that is connecting and reinforcing neurons needed to connect sounds and symbols. This hardwiring process is called orthographic mapping.

Let's quickly clarify the term "orthographic mapping." Sometimes this gets thrown around as an activity, or practice you do with kids. However, orthographic mapping is the cognitive process, or what is happening in the brain, when students are connecting spelling patterns and sounds. As this process is happening,

---

[3]Dehaene, S. 2010. *Reading in the Brain: The New Science of How We Read.* p. 224. (New York: Penguin Random House).

and the decoding connection becomes stronger and kids KNOW that word, we move that word into our sight word vocabulary. This is located in the MEANING portion of the reading brain.

This sight word vocabulary area is where we store all the words we have mapped and have made that sound–symbol connection. Now we know the word as if "by sight."

Eye-movement and brain research show that proficient readers still process every letter and connect sounds to symbols, but due to orthographic mapping, this happens at such a rapid rate (milliseconds) that we don't notice we are doing this. So, now when we see that word in text or anywhere, our brains automatically and effortlessly read that word. It does not need to slowly decode or connect the sound and letter patterns anymore, because we own that word. Adults have about 30,000–70,000 words in their sight word vocabulary! And that is our goal with phonics instruction … to get our kids to build their sight word vocabulary (not memorize "sight words").

Once students have more words stored in their sight word vocabulary, they now can shift their brain energy to understanding meaning from what they read (comprehension). They will no longer be struggling and using all their brain energy to try and decode words and now can focus on what the text is trying to tell them. These are all the wonderful things that are happening, in cohesion, within our reading brains for our kids to be able to read and comprehend. We hope this breakdown helps you understand more about the Reading Brain and what kids need to become successful readers!

When we are teaching phonics, we want to keep the reading brain in mind. Hearing the sound in a word and then knowing how it is spelled is going to be key for our students to be successful readers and writers. But we want to make sure not to leave out developing word meanings. This is beneficial, even while we are working on phonics. Meaning is a key part in helping kids own their words and comprehending what they read.

> "I used to think teaching Consonant, Vowel, Consonant (CVC) words was all about blending sounds into words (and that is a big part of it) but I missed the opportunities those words gave me to incorporate meaning! For example, if I am teaching the word 'BAT,' I typically just taught the word and moved on. But what an opportunity there to talk about the various meanings the word has. Am I talking about an animal that lives in a cave? Am I talking about the thing people swing in order to hit a ball?

Am I talking about an action? There is an opportunity—even at the earliest level of phonics—to teach word meanings and I don't want you to miss it!" —Heidi

So, how can we easily do this with our students? We created spelling riddles following our scope and sequence to help you incorporate all aspects of word learning—and make it fun!

These spelling riddles help kids work on phonics and spelling while incorporating all parts of the learning brain. The words follow our scope and sequence so kids are only working with phonics patterns they have learned (no more guessing!). They will use their sound knowledge and phonics knowledge to make the sound–symbol connections to spell each word.

While they continue working on their spelling skills, this activity was also created to work on enhancing and expanding children's background knowledge and vocabulary. This is a key component to helping create stronger and more competent readers. We not only need our students to be able to decode, spell, and read words fluently, but we also need them to understand what those words mean. This activity helps aid in that by providing clues, definitions, antonyms, and synonyms to build knowledge around the target word the kids are trying to spell. Each skill has approximately 5–10 words, depending on the skill. Yes, there might be a lot more words that connect to that specific spelling skill, but the word might be too advanced or does not have enough clues to help students reach the correct understanding or answer. This is why the number of words vary per skill.

The more information a child has about a word, the better equipped they are to remember, comprehend, and use that word.

# How to Use the Riddles

Print the sheet for the phonics skill you are working on. Students can use a white board, paper, or the recording sheet to write down their answers. Read them **one clue at a time**. *Encourage them to write down a guess after each clue!* This can be done in small groups, whole group, or one-on-one.

# Spelling Riddles

Cat
- I am an animal
- I live in the wild or can be a house pet
- I purr and meow
- I start with /k/

Bag
- I help you carry things
- You put things inside of me at stores
- I have two handles for you to hold while you carry me
- I start with /b/

Hat
- You wear me on your head
- Baseball players, cowboys, and police officers wear these on their heads for work
- I come in all shapes and colors
- I start with /h/

Bat
- I can live in a cave
- I sleep upside down and fly
- I am nocturnal, or only awake at night
- I eat insects and fruit
- I start with /b/
  OR
- I am made of wood or aluminum (metal)
- You swing me with your arms
- I am used to hit a ball in baseball
- I start with /b/

Ant
- I have six legs
- We crawl and like to follow each other
- I am a bug that lives in the ground, we dig tunnels underground
- I can be brown, black, or even red
- We are tiny, but very strong bugs
- We have a queen
- I start with /a/

# Spelling Riddles

Sad
- I am a feeling
- You can feel this when you lose something you love
- This feeling is the opposite of happy
- This feeling happens when you cry
- I start with /s/

Tag
- This is a game you can play
- You have to run around and try to touch people with your hand
- When someone touches you in this game, then you are it
- I start with /t/

Gas
- I am a liquid like water
- You put this inside cars, trucks, buses, and other transportation vehicles to make them go
- You have to go to a station to get me out of the pump
- I start with /g/

Map
- I am a piece of paper with roads, land, water, and places
- You use me to find how to get to different places
- I can be used to show you where different places are
- I was used by pirates to help them find treasure
- I start with /m/

Tap
- I use my finger to do this
- I can do this on someone's shoulder to get their attention or make them look at me
- This is like a small knock
- You might do this on your desk with your pencil
- (Demonstrate the motion for students)
- I start with /t/

# Spelling Riddles

Red
- • I am a color
- • I am the first color in a rainbow
- • I am the color of some apples
- • I am the color of a stop sign
- • I start with /r/

Ten
- • I am a number
- • You need two numbers to make me
- • I have a one and a zero
- • I come after nine
- • I start with /t/

Web
- • I am made of sticky string
- • I make cool designs
- • Spiders weave me to catch bugs
- • Spider-Man shoots me out his wrist to swing from the buildings
- • I start with /w/

Jet
- • I am fast and soar through the air
- • People fly me in the sky
- • I am another word for airplane
- • I start with /j/

Yes
- • I am a word used to agree with a question
- • I mean the same thing as moving my head in an up and down motion
- • I am the opposite of no
- • I start with /y/

@droppinknowledgewithheidi

# Spelling Riddles

Leg
- Most people have two of them
- They are used to help you move, walk, and run
- They are connected to your feet
- You use them to kick and jump
- I start with /l/

Wet
- This happens when you get water on you
- It is the opposite of dry
- I start with /w/

Bed
- This is a place where you sleep
- You will find this in a room
- You can have blankets and pillows on them
- You lay on this at night
- I start with /b/

Hen
- This is an animal from a farm
- It is the mother of baby chicks
- They cluck
- They can lay eggs
- I start with /h/

Net
- I am used to catch things
- I can help you catch bugs or fish
- This is what the ball goes through in basketball
- You can kick soccer balls into this to score
- I start with /n/

# Spelling Riddles

Sit
- You do this in a chair
- You are doing this when you are criss cross on the ground
- You can do this on a bench, couch, and in your desk
- I start with /s/

Win
- You do this when you beat a game
- If you score more points than the other team, you do this
- It is the opposite of lose
- I start with /w/

Lip
- This is on your face
- It is found under your nose
- It is part of your mouth
- You can kiss with this
- I start with /l/

Fin
- Fish use this to swim
- You can see this stick out of the top of water on sharks and dolphins
- This can be found on the back of airplanes
- I start with /f/

Pig
- I can be found on a farm
- I like to roll around in mud
- I make an oinking noise
- I start with /p/

@droppinknowledgewithheidi

# Spelling Riddles

Dip

- I am a food
- You use chips to scoop me out
- I have a lot of different flavors (queso, dill, French onion, salsa)
- I am usually at parties
- You can also dunk other foods in me
- I start with /d/

Rib

- I am a part of your skeleton
- I am lots of long bones in the middle of your body
- I protect your heart and lungs
- I can also be a type of barbeque food you eat
- I start with /r/

Mix

- This is when you combine a bunch of stuff together
- You can use a spoon to do this
- When you stir ingredients when making a cake, it is called this
- If you do this to red and yellow, you get orange
- I start with /m/

Big

- This is the size of something
- Elephants, dinosaurs, and tall buildings are this
- It is the opposite of small
- I start with /b/

Bib

- Babies wear these when they eat
- These help them not get messy
- It goes around their necks and covers their chest and stomach
- I start with /b/

@droppinknowledgewithheidi

# Spelling Riddles

Dog
- I am a pet
- I can be big or small and I am hairy
- I like to play fetch
- I bark and say Woof!
- I start with /d/

Mop
- I am a long pole with many floppy cotton strings at the end
- You dunk me in soapy water
- I'm used to clean up messes on the floor
- I start with /m/

Hot
- This is how it feels outside in the summer
- The desert weather feels like this all the time
- When you feel this, you start to sweat
- I start with /h/

Box
- You put stuff in me
- I am made of cardboard folded in a cube
- You use me to keep things safe if you send a gift to someone in the mail
- I start with /b/

Jog
- This is a movement
- This is also a way to get exercise
- This is faster than a walk, but slower than a run
- I start with /j/

# Spelling Riddles

Dot
- I'm a small solid circle
- I'm another name for the black spots on a ladybug
- You put me above the line when you write a lower case i
- I'm the shape of the period at the end of a sentence
- I start with /d/

Pop
- You can do this to a balloon to make it burst
- You eat this kind of corn when you go to the movies
- To also make a bubble burst you do this to it
- I start and end with /p/

Log
- I used to be a part of a tree
- I can be a home to many bugs and animals
- I'm the name of a piece of wood that lays on the floor in the forest
- I'm the name of a piece of wood floating in the water
- I start with /l/

Rob
- If you do this, you will get in trouble
- This is when you take something without asking
- It's another name for steal
- It can also be a person's first name
- I start with /r/

Fog
- This is a type of weather
- This usually happens in the night and early morning
- It's like all the clouds came down from the sky
- I make it really hard to see
- I start with /f/

@droppinknowledgewithheidi

# Spelling Riddles

Cub
- I am an animal
- I am brown, furry, and I growl
- I'm what you call a baby bear
- I start with /k/

Mud
- I can get you very dirty
- Pigs and other animals like to roll around in me to stay cool
- I'm what you get when you mix dirt and water
- I start with /m/

Bug
- I live outside
- I can fly and/or crawl
- I have six or eight legs
- I'm another name for an insect
- I am also the name, when someone keeps annoying you
- I start with /b/

Gum
- I'm a type of candy
- I'm a candy that you chew and chew, and can chew forever if you wanted
- I'm a candy that you do not swallow
- I can make your breath smell good
- I am in the middle of a Blow Pop sucker
- I start with /g/

Sun
- I am the star that all the planets go around
- I am extremely hot
- I give you the light to see during the day and help the plants grow
- I am the big yellow fiery ball that you see in the sky during the day
- I start with /s/

@droppinknowledgewithheidi

# Spelling Riddles

Cut
- This is what you do to paper with scissors
- You can get these on your skin and sometimes it will bleed
- You do this to food with a knife
- I start with /k/

Bus
- I am a really big vehicle
- A lot of people/kids ride on me to get places
- I'm the big yellow vehicle that takes kids to school
- I'm in a song where my wheels go round and round
- I start with /b/

Tub
- You find me in the bathroom
- I'm really big and you fill me up with water
- You can sit or stand in me to get your body clean
- I'm the part where the shower water sprays into
- I am another name for a bath
- I start with /t/

Hug
- This is a way to say hello sometimes
- People like to get these when they are sad or scared
- You do this with another person, when you both put your arms around each other
- I start with /h/

Nut
- I come from a tree
- I am a food
- Some people are allergic to me
- I am crunchy when you eat me as a snack
- I can be crushed and made into a butter that you like to eat with jelly
- Squirrels like to eat me and collect me for the winter
- I start with /n/

@droppinknowledgewithheidi

# Spelling Riddles

Math
- This is a subject that you do in school
- I am the subject that uses lots of numbers
- When you do this subject you learn about numbers, shapes, adding, and subtracting
- I start with /m/

Path
- I am like a small/mini road
- They have some of me for walking or biking
- I am a small road that you could follow through the forest
- I start with /p/

Thin
- This is when something is really skinny or not wide
- Paper is this
- I am the opposite of thick
- I start with /th/

Bath
- I am what you take a shower in
- I can also be called a tub
- You can fill me up with water and sit in me
- I am what you take when you need to get cleaned
- I start with /b/

Moth
- I am a flying insect
- I like to fly mostly at night
- I am like a butterfly but not as colorful
- I start with /m/

@droppinknowledgewithheidi

# Spelling Riddles

Ship
- I float on the water
- People travel on me to go on cruises
- I am also used to carry products for the store, by sailing through the ocean
- I am a boat, but a really big one
- I start with /sh/

Shop
- I am a store you can go to
- I am like a store but a smaller one
- If you go to stores and get things, I am what you're doing
- I start with /sh/

Cash
- I am green paper with different dollar amounts on them
- I am used to pay for and buy things
- I am another word for money
- I start with /k/

Shed
- I am usually found outside in people's yards
- I am a mini house
- People store or put things in me like tools, lawnmowers, or outdoor stuff
- I also am what snakes, lizards, and some bugs do to their skin when they grow bigger
- I start with /sh/

Fish
- I live in lakes, seas, and oceans
- I also can be a pet that needs a water tank
- I have scales and fins
- I swim around and breathe through my gills
- I start with /f/

@droppinknowledgewithheidi

# Spelling Riddles

Whip

- I am made of leather
- I am a long leather string with a handle
- I make a crack noise when you snap me through the air
- Horse racers use these to make their horses go faster
- Some cowboys have these and crack them for shows
- I start with /wh/

# Spelling Riddles

Chip
- I am a snack
- I am usually made from potatoes or corn
- I am crunchy
- I can be shaped like a circle, triangle, or rectangle
- You can also use me in dips
- Pringles, Doritos, Cheetos, and Takis are types of me
- I start with /ch/

Chin
- I am a part of your face
- I am the hard bone under your mouth at the bottom of your face
- You might put a strap under me to help hold on a helmet if you play sports
- I start with /ch/

Chop
- I am what you do with an ax to cut down a tree
- I am also the motion you use with a knife to cut up fruits and veggies
- People do this with their hand in karate
- I start with /ch/

Lunch
- I am in the meal that is in the middle of the day
- I come after breakfast and before dinner
- This is the time at school when you go to the cafeteria
- I start with /l/

Inch
- I am a measurement
- There are 12 of me on a ruler to equal one foot
- A quarter is about my size
- I start with /i/

@droppinknowledgewithheidi

# Spelling Riddles

King
- I am a part of royalty
- I can be the ruler of a place
- I usually live with a queen
- I wear a big shiny crown on my head
- I start with /k/

Bang
- This is the word when you hit something hard
- You do this on a drum with a drumstick
- Fireworks do this when they burst in the air
- I start with /b/

Long
- This is the size of something
- This is a word talking about length
- Kite strings, buses, and airplanes are this
- It is the opposite of short
- I start with /l/

Lung
- You have two of these inside your body
- It is the organ that helps you to breathe
- When you breathe in air, this is where the air goes inside your body
- I start with /l/

Ring
- This can be a piece of jewelry that you wear on your finger
- This is what the telephone does when someone calls
- You do this to a doorbell at someone's house
- I start with /r/

@droppinknowledgewithheidi

# Spelling Riddles

### Pass

- I am a movement
- You use your arm and hand to do this
- In sports it's what a quarterback does when they throw the ball
- Basketball and soccer players do this to get the ball to their teammates
- You get one of these when you are going to leave your class to go somewhere in the school
- I start with /p/

### Shell

- I come from lakes and oceans
- I am hard like a rock and give homes to sea creatures
- Clams and oysters live in these
- I start with /sh/

### Buzz

- I am a vibration sound
- This is the sound that bees and flies make when they fly
- If your phone is on vibrate, I can make this sound when it rings
- I start with /b/

### Hill

- I am a land feature
- Ants make these to get in their homes
- When the ground goes up, I make this
- I am like a mini mountain
- You have to walk up to get to the top of me
- I start with /h/

### Bell

- I am a something that makes a sound
- In music you can jingle me
- This is what you can ring to let someone know you are at their house
- This is what rings to tell you school is starting or ending
- I start with /b/

@droppinknowledgewithheidi

# Spelling Riddles

Stop
- I can be a big red sign you see on the street
- This means to not do what you're doing anymore
- I'm what you do at a red light
- I'm the opposite of go
- I start with /s/

Swing
- I am something you find at a playground
- You sit on me and go back and forth
- You might need a push from someone to help you get started on me
- Once you get going you use your legs to help you pump and get higher
- I start with /s/

Glass
- I am made from sand
- I am what some cups and dishes are made of
- The windows you look out of are made of this
- If you hit or drop me, I will break
- I start with /g/

Clap
- You do this with your hands
- You do this when you want to cheer someone on for doing a good job
- This is when you bring your two hands together again and again to make a noise
- I start with /k/

Brush
- I am a tool used to paint with
- I am something you use to comb your hair
- You do this to your teeth in this morning to make them clean
- I start with /b/

Frog
- I am an amphibian (I can live on land and in water)
- I am a green animal
- I like to hop to get places
- I can croak and ribbit to make noise
- I start with /f/

@droppinknowledgewithheidi

# Spelling Riddles

Pink
- I am a color
- If you mix red with white, you get me
- I am the color of your tongue
- I am the color of a flamingo
- I start with /p/

Bank
- I am a place
- I hold lots of money at my building
- You go to me when you want to get money
- You might have a piggy one of me to keep your money at home
- I start with /b/

Sink
- This is something that is in the kitchen and the bathroom
- It is an oval or rectangle shape and has a drain
- It is where the hot and cold water come out
- This is where you wash your hands or dishes
- It starts with /s/

Skunk
- I am an animal
- I usually live in the woods or near trees
- I am a black and white animal
- I shoot out a spray when I'm scared or trying to protect myself
- My spray stinks really really bad
- I start with /s/

Honk
- I am a noise
- Geese make this noise
- If you press the middle of the steering wheel in your car you can do this to a horn
- I start with /h/

# Spelling Riddles

Sock
- • I am a piece of clothing
- • I can be long or short
- • You put me on your feet, before you put on your shoes
- • I start with /s/

Clock
- • I help you tell time
- • I can be hanging on a wall or on your phone
- • I have hours and minutes
- • I start with /k/

Quack
- • I am a sound
- • I come from a bird
- • This is the sound a duck makes
- • I start with /k/ /w/

Sick
- • This is a bad feeling
- • When you are this, you can cough, sneeze, ache, and your stomach does not feel well
- • Sometimes when you feel like this you have to go to the doctor for medicine
- • I start with /s/

Pack
- • Something you do
- • You do this before you go on a trip
- • You do this when you put stuff in your suitcase
- • I start with /p/

@droppinknowledgewithheidi

# Spelling Riddles

Tape
- This is something sticky
- It can be clear, grey, or many other colors
- You use this to close and keep boxes together
- When wrapping a present, you use this to keep the wrapping paper on
- I start with /t/

Bike
- This is something you ride
- It can have one, two, three, or even four wheels
- You use pedals to make this go
- Kids love to ride these outside
- I start with /b/

Cone
- This is a 3D shape
- I look like a triangle with a circle on top
- This can be something orange to stop you from going into some place
- Party hats are in this shape
- This can be used to hold ice cream, and you can eat it too
- I start with /k/

Mute
- This means to silence or stop the talking or noise
- This is a button on your remote to turn off the volume
- You click this on your Zoom or your computer so people can't hear you talk
- I start with /m/

Wave
- This is something that can be found in the ocean or lake
- This is caused by wind and moving water
- This is when water gets tall and crashes into the beach or shore
- People surf on this with a surfboard
- This is something you do with your hand when you move it back and forth to say hello to someone
- I start with /w/

@droppinknowledgewithheidi

# Spelling Riddles

Dime
- This is a coin
- This is a silver or grey coin
- It is the smallest coin
- It is worth 10 cents
- I start with /d/

Bone
- This is something found inside your body
- These come in lots of different shapes and sizes
- Your skeleton has a lot of these
- Dogs like to chew on these
- I start with /b/

June
- This is one of the months of the year
- This month is the start of summer
- This month is after May and before July
- I start with /j/

Plane
- This is the name of a flat surface
- This is also a type of transportation
- This carries a lot of people to far places faster than driving
- This is something that flies in the air
- I start with /p/

Smile
- This is something you do with your mouth
- You do this by stretching out your lips and tightening your cheeks
- When you do this, it shows people you are happy
- I start with /s/

# Spelling Riddles

Ice
- This is something very cold
- You see this in the winter
- This is frozen water
- You can put this in your drink to cool it down
- I start with /i/ (long sound)

Cage
- This is something that is usually made out of metal
- This keeps things from getting out
- You can put pet birds in these or cats and dogs to take them places
- I start with /k/

Face
- This is what you call the round part of a clock
- This is also a part of your body
- This is located on your head
- This is where your eyes, nose, and mouth are at
- I start with /f/

Huge
- This is an adjective
- This is a word that means the opposite of small
- This word is like the word big
- This is to describe something that is really big
- I start with /h/

Space
- This can mean there is a lot of room
- This is located above us
- It is really dark here
- This is where you can find the satellites, stars, and planets
- I start with /s/

Spice
- This is something used in cooking
- Salt, pepper, and garlic are types of this
- You put this in food to make it taste better
- I start with /s/

Gem
- This is a mineral
- They are sparkly and shiny
- People use these in jewelry (necklaces, earrings, and rings)
- Diamonds, rubies, and emeralds are types of this
- I start with /j/

@droppinknowledgewithheidi

# Spelling Riddles

Bee
- This is an insect
- This insect can fly
- This insect is yellow and black
- They pollinate flowers and plants
- They make honey from the pollen they collect
- I start with /b/

Cheese
- This is a dairy food
- I can be in squares, shredded, or sticks
- You can melt me, and I get stretchy
- People say mice like to eat me
- I start with /ch/

Tree
- I am something that grows
- I can be small or grow really tall
- I have roots that suck up water to my trunk
- I have branches that have leaves
- Birds like to build nests on my branches
- I start with /t/

Queen
- I am a royal person
- I am in control of a place
- I live in a castle
- I can be married to a king
- I wear a beautiful jeweled crown
- I start with /qu/

Sheep
- I am an animal
- I can be found on a farm
- My puffy white hair is called wool
- Our babies are called lambs
- I start with /sh/

@droppinknowledgewithheidi

# Spelling Riddles

**Sheet**
- I am in the shape of a rectangle
- I can be a name for a piece of paper
- You can use me as a ghost costume
- I also am what you put on your bed and am like a thin blanket
- I start with /sh/

**Eel**
- I am a sea creature
- I hide and live in cracks in the coral and rocks of the ocean
- I am long like a snake
- I can shock you if you touch me
- I start with /ē/

**Seed**
- I am a small hard object in nature
- You can find me on the outside of strawberries and inside lemon
- Many people eat these from sunflowers
- You plant me in the soil in the ground
- I sprout and grow into plants and trees
- I start with /s/

**Feet**
- I am a part of your body
- You find me at the end of your legs
- I am used to help you walk and kick
- I have toes
- I start with /f/

**Green**
- I am a color
- I'm the color you get when you mix blue and yellow together
- I am the color of apples, grass, tree leaves, and frogs
- I start with /g/

# Spelling Riddles

**Vowel Team EA**

### Beach
- This is a place people like to go for vacation
- These are found near some lake but mostly oceans
- This is made of sand and where the waves crash onto
- I start with /b/

### Leaf
- These are part of plants
- This could also be a part of a dinner table
- You will find this at the end of a tree branch
- This can change colors in the fall
- Before winter trees get rid of this to save energy
- I start with /l/

### Dream
- This is something your brain thinks of
- People have these about something they hope to do in their life
- This is what happens when you are asleep in your brain
- These are like movies in your head when you sleep
- I start with /d/

### Clean
- This is something that helps keep you healthy
- This is a verb, so its something you do
- People do this to their houses
- You can even do this to your car to make it shiny again
- If you spill something this is what you do to get rid of the mess
- I start with /k/

### Eat
- This is something you need to do to survive
- This is a verb or something you do
- You use forks, spoons, or hands when you do this
- This is when you put food in your mouth
- I start with /ē/

# Spelling Riddles

**Vowel Team EA**

Beak
- I am a body part on a bird
- I am used as a tool to do a lot of things for a bird
- I can be big or small
- I am like the nose for a bird
- They also use me to eat
- I start with /b/

Steam
- I am created by water
- I look like smoke
- Some trains are powered by this
- This is what you get when water turns from a liquid to a gas
- This is what floats out of the pot when you boil water
- I start with /s/

Wheat
- This is a food crop
- When I grow, I am a golden/yellow color
- You grind me down and use me to make a lot of foods
- I am the main ingredient in bread, pasta, and cereal
- I start with /wh/

Meat
- This is a type of food
- I usually have a lot of protein
- If you are a vegetarian or vegan, you don't eat this
- Steak, chicken, turkey, and ham are types of me
- I start with /m/

East
- This is a direction
- If you look at a compass this is the direction on the left
- The sun rises from this direction
- I am the opposite of West
- I start with /ē/

@droppinknowledgewithheidi

# Spelling Riddles

Brain
- • This is found inside your body
- • This is in control of everything your body does
- • This helps you think when learning or doing something
- • This is located inside your head/skull
- • I start with /b/

Paint
- • This is something you can do in art class
- • This is also a supply you use in art
- • This involves lots of different colors
- • You use a brush to spread this liquid around
- • I start with /p/

Rain
- • I am part of the water cycle
- • This is what happens when small water molecules come together in a cloud
- • This happens usually when it is a cloudy dark sky
- • I am usually with thunder and lightning
- • This is what you call it when water falls from the sky
- • I start with /r/

Tail
- • This can be a part of an animal's body
- • They can be long or short
- • Animals use this to hang on things, swat bugs away, or to show they are happy
- • I am found at the back of an animal
- • I start with /t/

Train
- • This is a form of transportation
- • These carry people or supplies
- • I pull different cars
- • I can be electric, steam, or coal
- • I move on railroad tracks
- • I start with /t/

# Spelling Riddles

Mail
- This is how you send things to people
- I get picked up and dropped off by a person who works for the post office
- You put letters and packages in this type of box
- You put letters in an envelope with a stamp and send them through this
- I start with /m/

Maid
- This is a person
- This person works for people inside their house
- This person is in charge of cleaning everything in the house
- They are also sometimes in charge of watching and taking care of the kids
- I start with /m/

Bait
- This can be to get someone somewhere that you want them, like tricking them to go someplace
- This is also something that can be used to trap different animals
- You put this on a fishing hook to catch fish
- I start with /b/

Snail
- I am a gastropod
- I am slimy
- I have slimy body, with no legs or hands, and I slide places when I travel
- On my back I have a shell, that is my home
- I start with /s/

Drain
- This can mean to take out or away, without giving anything back
- This is what you do to pasta when it is done boiling
- This is the hole in your sink where the water flows down
- I start with /d/

@droppinknowledgewithheidi

# Spelling Riddles

Hay
- This is dried-up grass
- Farmers use machines to bail all of this dried grass into rectangular prisms
- Farmers use this to feed horses and other farm animals
- I start with /h/

Clay
- This is a material you use in art
- This material comes from the earth, and can be found underground
- This is soft and easy to squish and mold into things
- People use this to make pots, vases, and cups
- After you mold your creation, you cook it to make it hard
- I start with /k/

Spray
- This is something you do with liquids
- This is also what you call a small collection of branches
- Skunks do this when they are scared
- When you put a liquid in a bottle and pull the trigger this is what happens
- I start with /s/

May
- This is a month of the year
- It is during the start of summer
- It comes after April and before June
- I start with /m/

Day
- This has to do with the location of the sun
- This is when most living things are awake and active
- We can see the sun during this time
- This is the opposite of night
- I start with /d/

# Spelling Riddles

Boat
- This is a form of transportation
- This can have a motor or be rowed
- It floats on the water
- People fish off of these in the middle of lakes
- I start with /b/

Toad
- This is an amphibian
- I hop when I want to go places
- I am a brown color
- I eat insects
- I am different than a frog
- I start with /t/

Toast
- I am something you do to marshmallows to make s'mores
- People like to eat me in the morning for breakfast
- You can make me from bread
- If you put bread in a machine that heats it and then pops up you get me
- I start with /t/

Soap
- I am used for cleaning your body
- I can be a solid bar, liquid, or foam
- People use me to wash their hands
- I start with /s/

Coach
- This can also be something that is pulled by horses
- This is the head person on a team
- They come up with strategies to help teams win
- They tell you what to do at practice to help you get better
- I start with /k/

@droppinknowledgewithheidi

# Spelling Riddles

Coat
- This is a piece of clothing worn in cold conditions
- This goes on over your clothes and keeps your upper body and arms warm
- This can also sometimes be called a jacket
- I start with /k/

Throat
- I am a part of your body
- I am found in your neck
- This is where your vocal cords are to help you sing, talk, and make sounds
- When you are sick, I can become really sore
- I help you swallow things you eat and drink
- I start with /th/

Goal
- You can set or make one of these to help you achieve or get something you want
- This is also how you score points in some sports
- This can be a big net in soccer or a smaller one in hockey
- You try and put different objects in these to score points
- I start with /g/

Float
- This can be a dessert made of soda and ice cream
- This means you are buoyant, and do not sink
- Balloons filled with helium do this
- If a feather or leaf falls gently and slowly to the ground, they are doing this
- You can sit on tubes or rafts, or wear things on your arms in water to help you do this
- I start with /f/

Road
- This is something you travel on
- These can be made from dirt, asphalt, or cement
- Cars drive on these to get where they need to go
- Another word for this is a street
- I start with /r/

# Spelling Riddles

Bow
- This is something you can make out of ribbon
- You can wear these with a suit and is a type of tie
- This can also be a weapon you use to shoot an arrow
- You can find these on top of gifts
- I start with /b/

Grow
- This is something most living things do
- You do this as you get older
- Plants do this when they get water and sun
- This means to go from small to big
- I start with /g/

Pillow
- This is something that can be found on a bed
- This is something soft made from feathers or foam
- You use this to help you sleep
- This is what you put your head on when sleeping
- I start with /p/

Snow
- This is a type of weather
- This weather occurs during the winter months
- This is made from water that forms ice crystals
- You can build things with this and also have fights with this
- When there is a lot of this you have to plow or shovel
- I start with /s/

Window
- This is something that is part of your house and in vehicles
- This is made of glass
- These help you see out of your house and vehicle
- You can open these or roll these down to get air flow
- I start with /w/

@droppinknowledgewithheidi

# Spelling Riddles

Row
- This can mean a straight line of things
- This is also something you do with an oar
- This helps you move a boat with a paddle
- I start with /r/

Blow
- This is a movement of air
- You can do this with your mouth
- This is how you get air in a balloon
- You can do this to make bubbles
- I start with /b/

Crow
- These are a type of bird
- They are usually connected to spooky places
- They are black
- I start with /k/

Rainbow
- This is something found in nature
- This can be seen after a storm when the sun comes back out
- This is an arch across the sky
- This arch contains the colors Red, Orange, Yellow, Green, Blue, Indigo, and Violet
- I start with /r/

Mow
- This is something you have to do to a yard
- You do this when your grass gets long
- You use a machine to cut your grass low again
- I start with /m/

@droppinknowledgewithheidi

# Spelling Riddles

Night
- This is connected to the Earth orbiting the sun
- A lot of animals are awake during this time
- When the sun sets it becomes this
- This is the opposite of day
- I start with /n/

High
- This word is an adjective
- It can be used to describe a hill or mountain
- Can be used in weather to say what the max temperature for the day will be
- This is the opposite of low
- I start with /h/

Tight
- You wrap things like this so they do not come loose
- This is how you hold on to something so you do not fall or drop it
- Can be a spot that is difficult for someone or something to pass through
- This is how your shoes feel when your feet are too big
- I start with /t/

Right
- This can be a direction
- Can mean that you agree with someone
- Can be a law that is given to everyone
- This is the opposite of left
- I start with /r/

Thigh
- This is a muscle
- You find this muscle on your legs
- You can get a charlie horse or muscle cramp here
- This muscle is between your knee and your hip
- I start with /th/

Bright
- This is something you can see with your eyes
- When this happens, you tend to block or squint your eyes
- This can be a color that really pops or stands out
- The sun is this, that's why you can't stare at it
- If you are in a dark room and someone turns on the light it becomes this
- I start with /b/

# Spelling Riddles

**Fall**
- This is one of the four seasons
- This is something you do if you trip
- Leaves turn red, yellow, orange, and brown during this season
- When the leaves break off the tree, they do this to get to the ground
- I start with /f/

**Pull**
- This is a verb or an action
- This is a way to tear things apart
- You do this to open a door
- This action will help you win a tug of war
- I start with /p/

**Ball**
- This is a round object
- This can be a fancy dinner and dance party
- You use these in almost all sports
- I start with /b/

**Full**
- This is to fill up something until there is no more room
- Can also mean having lots of flavor within something you eat
- You can feel this way when you eat a lot of food
- This is the opposite of empty
- I start with /f/

**Ill**
- This can be a feeling your body has
- This is what happens when you get a virus or bacteria inside you
- This is another word for feeling sick
- I start with /ĭ/

@droppinknowledgewithheidi

# Spelling Riddles

Grill
- This cooks food
- This can also mean to ask a lot of questions
- You find and use this cooking device outside
- You can use propane gas or charcoal to start the fire
- I start with /g/

Wall
- This is part of a building
- You use 3 or more of these to make a room
- People hang things on these to decorate their house
- You put windows in these to be able to see outside
- I start with /w/

Bull
- This is an animal
- These animals can have long pointy horns
- They are herbivores which means they like to eat plants
- These are male cows
- I start with /b/

Gill
- This is a body part of a fish
- These are the slits or lines on the side of a fish's head
- These help the fish breathe
- I start with /g/

Drill
- This is a tool
- It can also mean making a hole in something
- You can also do this to practice something
- This tool can is electric or battery powered
- This tool can be used to put a screw in different materials
- I start with /d/

@droppinknowledgewithheidi

# Spelling Riddles

Cold
- This can be a feeling
- You feel this when the temperature gets lower
- When you are sick, people say that you "caught a ___"
- This is the opposite of hot
- I start with /k/

Bolt
- This can mean to run somewhere quickly and suddenly
- This can also be a metal piece that can be screwed in to hold materials together
- This is also what you see when lightning strikes
- I start with /b/

Gold
- This is a metal
- This metal is shiny
- This metal can be worth lots of money
- This is the medal that is given for coming in first place
- I start with /g/

Fold
- This is a verb or an action
- You bend or crease something when you do this
- People do this to their laundry
- You do this to paper when you bend it to hot dog or hamburger style
- I start with /f/

Blind
- This can be something you put on to cover windows and close them so no one can see in your house
- This can also be a hidden box used to hide when hunting
- This can also refer to someone who cannot see
- I start with /b/

@droppinknowledgewithheidi

# Spelling Riddles

AR Words

Car
- This is a form of transportation
- This can also be part of a train
- This has four wheels
- You drive this to get to places
- I start with /k/

Farm
- This is a location
- At this place they can grow lots of things like corn, pumpkins, wheat, fruits, and vegetables
- This place sometimes has a big red barn
- This place also usually has lots of animals like cows, ducks, horses, sheep, and goats
- I start with /f/

Star
- This is something we see in outer space
- This can also be someone who is really good at their job
- This is also a shape with 5 points
- There are billions of these in our solar system
- These glow and twinkle at night
- I start with /s/

Shark
- This is a sea creature
- There are many different types of these in the ocean
- These are predators and hunt other fish and sea life
- These sea animals have thousands of sharp teeth
- Some of the most known types of these are great whites and hammerheads
- I start with /sh/

Park
- This is location you can go to
- This is also something you can do to a car when you get somewhere
- This place usually has lots of grass for you to run around
- This place also has lots of stuff to play on like swings, slides, and monkey bars
- I start with /p/

# Spelling Riddles

**AR Words**

### March
- This is something people can do, usually they are in a line and lift their knees and legs up high when they move forward
- This is also a month of the year
- This is the month that is typically the start of spring
- This month comes right after February
- I start with /m/

### Arm
- This is a part of your body
- This body part starts at your shoulder and goes to your hand
- You use this body part to throw or lift something
- I start with /ar/

### Scarf
- This is a piece of clothing
- This can also mean to eat your food very quickly
- This is something you wear during the winter to help keep warm
- This piece of clothing is usually long
- You wrap this around your neck and face to keep you warm
- I start with /s/

### Yarn
- This is a twisted strand of rope, usually made from wool or cotton
- This is what people use to knit or weave
- This comes in many different colors and can be wound up in a ball
- When people use this in knitting it is to make things like blankets, scarfs, or hats
- I start with /y/

### Sharp
- This is an adjective or describing word
- This is something that is very pointy
- This means it can poke or cut you really easily
- This can also be a pain you feel that is intense and quick
- We like our scissors and knives to be like this to cut through stuff easily
- This is the opposite of dull
- I start with /sh/

# Spelling Riddles

Under
- This is a positional word
- This means to be below something
- This word is the opposite of over
- I start with /ŭ/

Paper
- This is made from trees
- This can be used to wrap things
- The main thing this is used for is for people to write on
- You sometimes use a pencil to write on this
- I start with /p/

Number
- These are used for counting
- These help describe how much of something
- You can use these in different ways in math ... Add them, subtract them
- I start with /n/

Tiger
- This is an animal
- This animal is part of the big cat family
- This animal tends to live in the jungles or forests
- This animal is orange with black stripes
- I start with /t/

Lobster
- This is a sea creature
- This is a crustacean sea creature, which means it has a hard shell
- This sea creature can be red, black, or blue
- This creature has two big pinchers but is not a crab
- I start with /l/

# Spelling Riddles

**OR Words**

Corn
- This is a type of grain or vegetable
- This grows from a tall stalk
- You can eat this on the cob or in little individual pieces
- This can also be dried and popped as a snack that you usually get from the movies
- I am the color yellow
- I start with /k/

Fork
- This is an eating utensil
- This can also be where two roads split in different directions
- This is long with little spikes at the end
- We used this utensil to poke food and be able to bring it to your mouth
- I start with /f/

North
- This is a direction
- A compass needle always points this direction
- This is usually the direction that points to the top of the map
- This is the opposite of South
- I start with /n/

Horn
- This can be a long part that sticks out of an animal's head like a rhino
- This can also be a crescent moon shaped piece of land
- This can also be a musical instrument that's part of a band
- Vehicles have these as well and you can honk them
- I start with /h/

@droppinknowledgewithheidi

# Spelling Riddles

Torch
- This can mean to light something on fire
- These were used as a light source in ancient times
- This is a long stick with a flame on the end that you can carry and move
- I start with /t/

Sport
- This is something you can play
- This involves different movement and skills to play
- Basketball, baseball, tennis, football, soccer, and golf are all types of this
- I start with /s/

Cord
- This is a long and thin piece of twisted yarn or rope
- Can also be a measurement for a stack of firewood
- This is the long piece of wire that you plug in to get power
- I start with /k/

Porch
- This is a part of a house
- You can have these in the front or back of your house
- It connects and extends right by your front or back door
- Sometimes referred to as a stoop
- This is an area where you can sit
- I start with /p/

@droppinknowledgewithheidi

# Spelling Riddles

Bird
- • This is an animal
- • These animals travel mainly by flying
- • Some types of these are flightless like emus or ostriches
- • These animals build nests for their eggs
- • I start with /b/

Dirt
- • This is part of the earth
- • You can dig this out of the ground
- • This is brown and black
- • You use this to help plants grow; sometimes called soil
- • I start with /d/

Shirt
- • This is a piece of clothing
- • There are short, long, and sweat types of this
- • This piece of clothing goes on the upper half of your body
- • You put your head and arms in this to cover your stomach and chest
- • I start with /sh/

Stir
- • This word is often a motion
- • This word means to combine things together
- • This can also mean to disrupt something
- • This is another word for mix
- • I start with /s/

Circus
- • This is a traveling group of performers
- • This can also mean something that is noisy, wild, and chaotic
- • They usually have this under a red-and-white tent
- • This group of performers often include acrobats and clowns
- • I start with /s/

@droppinknowledgewithheidi

# Spelling Riddles

Burp
- This is caused by a buildup of gas in your body
- This is something you have to do to babies after they eat
- This can be a loud sound
- This happens when you release or let go of the gas through your mouth
- I start with /b/

Surf
- This is an activity
- You do this at a beach
- You need a board to stand on to do this
- This can also mean a breaking wave
- I start with /s/

Burn
- This can mean to cover with flames and turn black
- Can also be when someone says something mean to someone and it hurts their feelings
- You can get one of these if you touch something extremely hot
- I start with /b/

Nurse
- This is an occupation or job
- This person works in hospitals
- This person works with doctors to help treat patients
- I start with /n/

Turn
- This means to change direction
- You can do this to make something go on or off
- If you are driving a car you do this to make the car go right or left
- I start with /t/

@droppinknowledgewithheidi

# Spelling Riddles

Happy
- This is a feeling
- You feel this when good things are happening to you
- This feeling makes people smile and laugh
- This is the opposite of sad
- I start with /h/

Bunny
- This is an animal
- This animal lives in a burrow
- This animal hops to travel
- It can also be called a rabbit
- I start with /b/

Baby
- This is a very young human or animal
- This needs parents or someone/thing to raise it
- This cries a lot to communicate
- This can also be called a newborn
- They sleep in a crib and drink out of a bottle
- I start with /b/

City
- This is a place
- Many people live here
- These usually have large buildings and a lot of things going on
- Sometimes can be called an urban area
- New York and Chicago are these
- I start with /s/

@droppinknowledgewithheidi

# Spelling Riddles

Windy
- This is a type of weather
- This means the air is in motion
- When it is one of these days, things tend to blow everywhere
- I start with /w/

Candy
- This is a sweet treat
- These are made with sugar
- These can be hard, chewy, sweet, sour, or chocolatey
- Some types of this are lollipops, gummy bears, chocolate bars
- I start with /k/

Family
- This is a group of people
- This group of people are often related to each other
- This can include parents, aunts, uncles, brothers, sisters, or close friends
- I start with /f/

Lazy
- This means to not do anything or not put in effort
- This can also mean move very slowly
- If you are this, you do not help out with things
- This is the opposite of active or energetic
- I start with /l/

@droppinknowledgewithheidi

# Spelling Riddles

Zoo
- This is a place
- At this place you can explore different habitats
- This place has many animals for you to see and learn about
- Some animals are elephants, lions, alligators, and monkeys
- I start with /z/

Spoon
- This is an eating utensil
- This utensil has a round end
- This can help you stir stuff together
- This helps you eat soup or cereal
- I start with /s/

Roof
- This is a part of a house or building
- This part of the house usually has shingles to protect it from rain
- This part of the house or building is usually slanted
- This is the top of the house
- I start with /r/

Broom
- This is a cleaning tool
- This is also something they say witches or wizards ride
- You use this to clean up messes on the floor
- You collect the stuff on the floor by sweeping with this
- I start with /b/

Tooth
- This is a part of your body
- You find these in your head
- This starts as a baby, then you lose it, and grow a bigger one
- This is found in your mouth
- The name of one of these starts with /t/

# Spelling Riddles

Pool
- This is a place or thing to do in the summer or to have fun
- Some of these are above the ground and some are in the ground
- You can have waterslides that go into this
- This is what you swim and play in
- I start with /p/

Igloo
- This is a winter home
- Many indigenous Inuit people built these to live in the cold frost tundra
- This is a dome-shaped house
- This house is made from bricks of snow
- I start with /ĭ/

Root
- This can be a type of vegetable
- This is also something all plants have
- These are long strands that dig deep into the ground
- This is what sucks up the water from the ground to feed the plant
- I start with /r/

Moon
- This is an object in the sky
- This object goes through different phases every month
- Sometime this is full or whole and sometimes you cannot see this at all
- This is the big glowing ball or crescent we see at night
- I start with /m/

Balloon
- This is an inflatable object
- Some types of these can be twisted into animal shapes or other cool objects
- They have water types of these you can fill up and throw with your family and friends
- To inflate this object, you can use helium or blow it up using your breath
- Many people have these at birthday parties or celebrations
- I start with /b/

@droppinknowledgewithheidi

# Spelling Riddles

Book
- This is used to tell a story or facts
- There are many types of this; some are hardback and some are paperback
- You read these
- You can find lots of these at the library
- I start with /b/

Wood
- This comes from a tree
- You use a saw or ax to chop or cut this
- You can use this to build houses and furniture
- This is also something you can use to start a campfire or a fire in a fireplace
- I start with /w/

Hook
- This is a curved shape
- This can be used to hang things on like coats or plants
- This can also be the catchy and repetitive part of a song
- This is also used at the end of fishing line to catch a fish
- I start with /h/

Foot
- This is a part of your body
- This is connected to your leg
- You use this to help you balance and walk
- This part of your body is where your toes are connected to
- I start with /f/

Cook
- This can be a job
- This can also be a verb or something you do
- This person works at a restaurant
- They are the ones who make the food for you
- You do this to food in the kitchen when you want it hot and to eat it
- I start with /k/

Wool
- This is something that clothes can be made out of
- Some yarn is made from this material
- You get this from sheep; it's what their hair is called
- I start with /w/

@droppinknowledgewithheidi

# Spelling Riddles

Saw
- This is a tool
- This can also mean you looked at something with your eyes
- This can also be a motion back and forth
- You use this tool to cut wood in half
- I start with /s/

Fawn
- This is a baby animal
- This can also be a color
- This animal lives in the forest
- Some of these animals grow up and have antlers
- This is what a baby deer is called
- I start with /f/

Yawn
- This is a verb or action word
- This is when you open your mouth wide and take a deep breath
- You do this when you are bored or sleepy
- I start with /y/

Claw
- This is a part of some animal's bodies
- This is also a tool used to grip and hold things
- Lobster and crabs have these as hands
- Birds use these to capture fish or perch on tree branches
- I start with /k/

Straw
- This is dried-up wheat that farmers use in their animal's beds and in their barns
- This can also be a yellowish color
- This is also a device you use to suck up liquids from a cup when you drink
- I start with /s/

# Spelling Riddles

Crawl
- This is a verb or action
- This can mean to move very slowly like in a traffic jam
- Insects do this like spiders in a web
- When you do this, you are on your hands and knees and moving
- I start with /k/

Draw
- This is something you do in art
- When you do this, you can use markers, pencils, or pens
- This is a way to create a picture
- I start with /d/

Seesaw
- This is a piece of playground equipment
- This requires two people
- Each person sits on opposite sides
- When one person goes up the other goes down and this repeats
- I start with /s/

Jaw
- This is a part of your body
- This is the part of the body that connects to your mouth and teeth
- This is the bone that moves your mouth to chew or talk
- I start with /j/

Dawn
- This can be someone's name
- This can also mean that you just remembered or figured something out
- This also relates to a time of day
- This is the time of day when the sun is just coming up
- I start with /d/

# Spelling Riddles

August
- This is a month of the year
- This month is a summer month
- This month comes right after July and before September
- I start with /au/

Sauce
- This is a food
- These are liquid foods to help add flavor
- You put these on different vegetables and meats before cooking or to use as a dip
- Some types of these are barbeque, tomato, soy, and buffalo
- I start with /s/

Pause
- This means to take a break or have a stop in the action
- This can also mean to hesitate from doing something
- This is a button you can find on a remote or game shown by two straight lines next to each other
- I start with /p/

Launch
- This is an action
- You can do this to get a boat from a dock to water
- This also means to move with force
- This is how you get a rocket into space … 5.4.3.2.1
- I start with /l/

Author
- This word is connected to books
- This is the person who thinks of what to write
- This is also the person who creates the book
- You find their names on the front cover of books
- I start with /au/

# Spelling Riddles

Cow
- This is an animal
- This animal is usually black and white, but can also be brown
- This animal produces milk
- This animal is often found on farms: "MOO"
- I start with /k/

Down
- This is a direction
- This is also a cluster of feathers to keep ducks and geese warm
- When you fall this is the direction you go
- This is the opposite of up
- I start with /d/

Owl
- This is a type of bird
- This bird is nocturnal or awake at night
- This is a bird of prey
- This bird's feathers are silent when the fly to help with hunting
- This bird is said to hoot
- I start with /ow/

Plow
- This is a way farmers prepare their fields to begin to plant
- Farmers put these on tractors to break up the dirt
- This can mean to run over or through something
- This is a tool you can put on trucks to clear snow on roads
- I start with /p/

Crown
- This can mean the top of something like of your head, a hill, or a tree
- This is also a sign of royalty
- This is made to wear on the head often with gold and diamonds
- Many queens and kings wear these
- I start with /k/

@droppinknowledgewithheidi

# Spelling Riddles

Power
- This can mean to be able to rule or control someone or something
- This can also mean to have a lot of force to move something
- Electricity is a form of this to make things turn on
- This can mean to give things energy or turn things on
- I start with /p/

Clown
- This is a type of artist
- This is also a costume many people dress up as
- This character or performer is usually found in a circus
- This performer wears makeup with a big red nose and acts silly
- I start with /k/

Frown
- This is a facial expression
- This usually shows displeasure or sadness
- This is the opposite of a smile
- I start with /f/

Howl
- This is a sound
- This can be a sound of pain
- Many wolves do this to communicate
- I start with /h/

Flower
- This is a type of plant
- These plants come in many shapes and colors
- Bees collect pollen and nectar from these plants
- These plants often have a good smell
- I start with /f/

@droppinknowledgewithheidi

# Spelling Riddles

Mouth
- This is a part of your body
- This is where your teeth are located
- Your tongue is found in here
- I start with /m/

House
- This is a place
- This place has lots of different rooms
- These can also be a toy/play place for dolls
- This place has kitchens, bedrooms, and living rooms
- I start with /h/

Couch
- This is something you sit on
- It is a comfortable piece of furniture
- You usually find this in the living room
- This is a seat that can fit more than one person
- I start with /k/

South
- This is a direction
- This direction usually points to the bottom of a map
- This is the opposite of North
- I start with /s/

Pouch
- This can be a small bag to carry something
- This is also a part of a kangaroo
- This is the place where a baby marsupial or kangaroo is carried by their mother
- I start with /p/

# Spelling Riddles

Mouse
- This is a type of rodent
- This rodent is small
- This can also be part of a computer that you move with your hand to click on stuff
- These rodents have whiskers and big ears
- These are said to like cheese
- I start with /m/

Cloud
- This is something we see in the sky
- There are different types of these such as cirrus, cumulus, stratus, and nimbus
- These are made from billions of tiny droplets of water
- When they get full of water, they release rain
- I start with /k/

Out
- This means to be away from or not there
- This is also a part of baseball when a ball is caught, or a runner gets tagged
- It can be when a pitcher throws three strikes to a batter
- This is the opposite of in
- I start with /ou/

Loud
- This is a noise
- This noise is at a high pitch or intensity
- This type of noise can make you cover your ears
- This is the opposite of quiet
- I start with /l/

Sour
- This is a taste
- This can also be when a food spoils or becomes old
- There are candies that have this taste
- Lemons and limes have this taste
- This is the opposite of sweet
- I start with /s/

@droppinknowledgewithheidi

# Spelling Riddles

Coin
- This is a type of money
- These are round
- They come in different amounts
- These are mostly silver, but can also be copper or gold
- The amounts can be 1, 5, 10, or 25 cents
- I start with /k/

Oil
- This is a liquid
- This can be something that needs to get changed and put in your car to help it run
- This is also something you can use to hydrate or moisturize your skin
- This is also something used to cook with
- A lot of fried foods are cooked in this
- I start with /oi/

Point
- This can mean the sharp end of a stick or pencil
- This can also be the topic of a discussion or debate you are having
- This can be a specific location on a map
- You get these in sports and games when you make a basket, run, or get an answer correct
- This is something you do when you stick your finger out at someone or at a direction
- I start with /p/

Boil
- This can be a bump on the skin you get from an infection
- This can also be a name for a group of hawks
- This is also when water starts to become a vapor
- This is what happens when you heat up water at a high temperature and bubbles start to pop up
- I start with /b/

# Spelling Riddles

Joint
- This can mean to have two or more people working together or sharing something
- This is also part of your body
- These are the places in your body where two bones come together usually to help you move or bend
- Examples of these are you shoulder, knee, ankle, and elbow
- I start with /j/

Soil
- This is part of the earth
- This can also mean to soak or get something extremely dirty
- This is found in the ground
- This has lots of nutrients that help plants grow
- A synonym for this word is dirt
- I start with /s/

Coil
- This can be an action to wind something up often in a spiral
- This can also be spiral wire used to move electricity
- This is a piece of equipment or material that is wound in a helix or spiral
- I start with /k/

Voice
- This is something created in your body
- This can also mean to speak up or share your opinion
- This is what you use to communicate
- This is the sound that is created from your throat to help you talk
- I start with /v/

@droppinknowledgewithheidi

# Spelling Riddles

OY
Words

Boy
- This is a person
- A synonym for this is male
- This is the opposite of a girl
- I start with /b/

Destroy
- This is a verb
- This can mean to get rid of completely
- This is a form of destruction or breaking something down
- I start with /d/

Toy
- This is an object
- This is something you play with
- This can be an action figure, doll, cars, plastic animals, or even a teddy bear
- Kids love to get these as presents
- I start with /t/

Cowboy
- This is a person
- These people usually live on a farm or ranch
- They are known to be from old western movies
- They like to wear hats, ride horses, and sometimes can even lasso
- They are in charge of running a ranch and moving cattle or cows from one place to another
- I start with /k/

Oyster
- This is a sea creature
- They are part of the mollusk family
- These tend to stick themselves to rocks
- Some types of these create pearls
- Some people enjoy eating these
- I start with /oy/

# Spelling Riddles

Banana
- This is a tropical fruit
- This fruit grows in a long, curved shape
- This fruit grows in bunches
- This is a yellow fruit
- I start with /b/

Camel
- This is an animal
- This animal lives in desert climates
- This animal has four legs and fur
- This animal has humps on its back
- This animal can store water in its humps to help it survive in a dry climate
- I start with /k/

Present
- This can be a word that means right now
- This can also mean a gift that you give someone
- You give these to people to celebrate an event like a birthday
- These are usually wrapped in wrapping paper and can have bows
- I start with /p/

Blanket
- This can mean to cover something
- This is also something that you use to cover yourself to keep warm
- This is a large piece of fabric that you wrap around yourself
- This is usually used when you are laying on a couch or to cover yourself when you go to sleep to keep warm
- I start with /b/

Pencil
- This is a writing tool
- This is made of wood
- The tip of this has lead that you sharpen to write with
- I start with /p/

# Spelling Riddles

**Schwa Words**

Soda
- This is a liquid
- This is something you drink
- This has bubbles, or carbonation, inside it
- This is a sweet drink
- They have lots of types of this like Coke, Sprite, or root beer
- I start with /s/

Cactus
- This is a plant
- This plant is found in desert climates
- This plant does not need a lot of water to grow
- This plant can produce flowers
- This plant has spikes that are really sharp
- I start with /k/

Salad
- This is a food item
- This food can have lots of different things in it
- Many of the ingredients are raw vegetables
- The main ingredients of this food are lettuce, tomato, and sliced carrots
- You usually put a dressing on this like ranch, vinaigrette, Italian, or French
- I start with /s/

Africa
- This is a huge land mass
- This is one of our 7 continents
- This continent has many different climates ranging from deserts to huge tropical jungles
- This continent is located below the Western part of Europe and stretches down to almost Antarctica
- Some countries of this continent are Madagascar, Cameroon, Nigeria, and Egypt
- I start with /ă/

Pilot
- This is an occupation or job
- This can also mean the first episode of a new show
- This can also mean a test to see if something works
- This person is in control of flying an airplane
- I start with /p/

# Let's Talk About Spelling Tests

During Heidi's first year of teaching, she gave weekly spelling tests. As we told you earlier, she actually stopped teaching spelling after this. But even thinking back on the tests she gave her students that first year, she realized that the words she tested her kids on were completely random. There was no rhyme or reason for the words she was using:

> "I remember one time I tested my kids on all the Vowel-R words . . . all at once (ER, AR, OR, IR, and UR)! At that time, I had not explicitly taught those phonics skills to my students. There are two problems here. One, testing all of those skills at once is overwhelming for students. Two, if I have not explicitly taught these phonics patterns, how could I test them on those words? These are those cringey moments I look back on and just wish I had known better!"

Adam's experience was very similar. He took words given by the curriculum to have the students practice throughout the week and then test them on Friday. Those words did not revolve around a specific skill and/or were too advanced for the majority of his students, due to the fact that there was no specific phonics instruction incorporated within the curriculum. Phonics was a supplement and afterthought, unfortunately.

When we give kids a list of spelling words to practice for the week, test them on Friday, and then move on, we essentially ask them to memorize those words for a short period. Since this is not aligned with how our brains learn to read, kids will forget these words the following week.

It can also be problematic to test kids on words that have phonics patterns that have not been explicitly taught yet. When we do this, we ask kids to memorize words and spelling patterns. Neuroscience shows us that we do not learn to read by memorizing words as a whole.

Cognitive Neuroscientist Stanislas Dehaene says that whole word reading is a myth. He says that as adults, we have the illusion that we are reading whole words because our brains get lightning fast at matching sounds to symbols. But he emphasizes that this is an illusion, and we are still reading by matching those sounds to symbols. He also discusses how this looks different in kindergarten and first grade. Kids are much slower at this, so if you are a teacher or a parent of a kindergartener or a first-grade student who is laboriously blending words sound by sound, just know that is part of the development of learning how to read.

"As expert reading adults, we systematically underestimate how difficult it is to read, The words given to beginning readers must be analyzed letter by letter in order to ensure that they do not contain spelling problems that are beyond the child's current knowledge—for instance, unusual pronunciations, silent letters, double consonants, or peculiar endings such as the suffix "-tion." All of these peculiarities, if they are introduced too early in the curriculum, can make children think that reading is arbitrary and not worth studying. As a scientist and a professor myself, I expect the teachers and educators to whom I entrust my children to invest as much obsessive care in the design of lessons as my colleagues and I do when we prepare a psychological experiment."[4]

So then, how should we teach spelling?

**We should align our spelling words with the phonics skills we teach.**
For example, if I am teaching the vowel team -EA during our phonics lessons, then my spelling words for that week should be words with the spelling pattern -EA. If I'm teaching digraphs, my spelling words should be words with digraphs. It is important here to follow a scope and sequence so you're not accidentally testing kids on words with phonics patterns you haven't taught yet. Digraphs are taught before silent E words in a typical scope and sequence. You should be careful that when you test your kids on words with digraphs, you are not including words like shake or phone because kids have yet to learn that Consonant, Vowel, Consonant, E (CVCE) pattern.

**We should give our kids different words for practice than the words we will assess them on.**
If we give kids the set of words that we will test them on, they are likely to practice memorizing the shape of the word, look of the word, spelling of the word, and this is what we want to avoid. We really want our kids to focus on this phonics skill and how to spell using that specific phonics pattern. A simple way to do this is to give kids practice words with the phonics pattern we are focusing on. The practice words will be different from those we will assess at the end of the week. This ensures that the kids are

[4]Dehaene, S. 2010. *Reading in the Brain: The New Science of How We Read.* p. 230. (New York: Penguin Random House).

really practicing their words by matching sounds to symbols and focusing on that phonics pattern.

**We should have kids practicing their spelling words through phoneme-grapheme mapping.**

This is a reminder that a phoneme is a sound, and a grapheme are the letter or letters that spell each sound. So when kids are working on their words for the week, we don't want to give them practice activities where they're focusing on the shape of the word or the look of the word in any way. We want them to practice these words in a way that aligns with how our brains read, and that is by matching sounds to symbols or phonemes to graphemes. This is one of the most efficient practices we can do with our kids to help them strengthen those connections between the front and back of our reading brain, and get them to learn those new phonics patterns.

# Remember the Reading Brain?

The **Simple** View
of the
Reading Brain

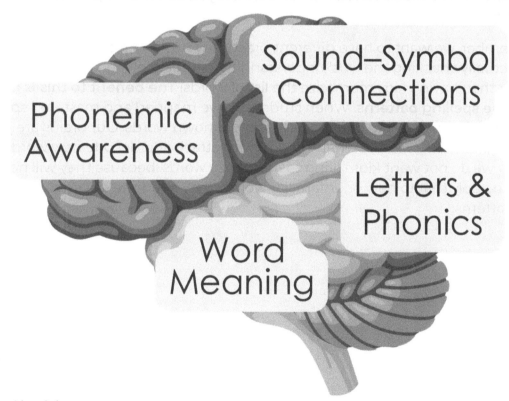

Sound–Symbol
Connections

Phonemic
Awareness

Letters &
Phonics

Word
Meaning

droppinknowledge.com

All of these parts must **work together**
in order for us to read!

**When our brains read, we are connecting sounds to symbols**. When we start our lessons with phonemic awareness, we activate our phonological processor (the part of our brains that processes sounds), and then we want to connect those sounds to the letters that represent them. This allows that orthographic mapping process to happen when our brain begins to make those cognitive neuron connections to help it solidify the understanding of that skill.

The following pages include spelling practice words and challenge words for each phonics skill[5] in the scope and sequence. There is a practice spelling page with sound boxes that can be used for all phonics skills. We recommend putting this page in a sheet protector or laminating it to be used over and over again.

We have also included various spelling sheets you can use for practice and testing.

Remember, we want to have different practice words and test words. This way we are actually checking the kids' understanding of that spelling and phonics skills rather than having kids memorize the list of words! **The benefit to this is mastery of these spelling patterns.** When students have mapped and mastered spelling patterns, they use this to decode new and unknown words. Our brains are pattern seeking, and they will use what they know to attack and decode new words. This is why we do not want kids trying to memorize words, because they will not be able to apply that to new or unfamiliar words. They need the skills and mastery of the patterns.

---

[5]Please note—Several skills have only five words for practice and testing. This is because we are following our scope and sequence and do not want to give kids words with phonics skills they have not yet learned. This limits the number of words we are able to use. There is not a set for -UE words as there are too few words available.

# Spelling Practice Page

Say the word.
Have the child repeat the word.
Have them say & count each sound in the word.
Choose which boxes you will use to map the word.
Say and spell each sound one at a time.

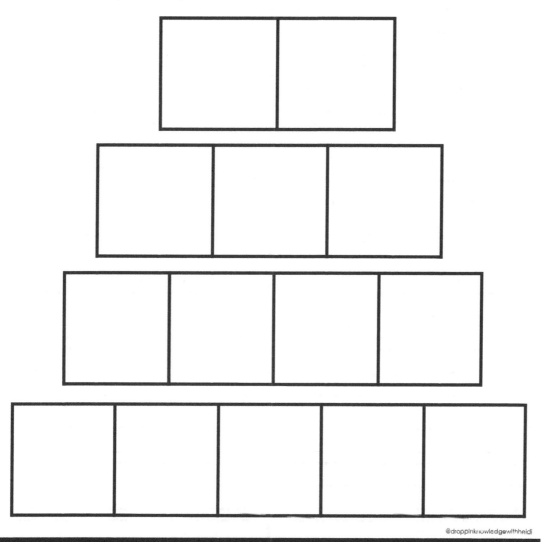

@droppinknowledgewithheidi

# Spelling

## Practice Words

# Spelling

## Practice Words

# Spelling

## Practice Words

# Spelling

## Practice Words

# Spelling

## Practice Words

|  |  |  |  |
|--|--|--|--|
|  |  |  |  |
|  |  |  |  |
|  |  |  |  |
|  |  |  |  |
|  |  |  |  |
|  |  |  |  |
|  |  |  |  |
|  |  |  |  |
|  |  |  |  |

# Spelling

## Practice Words

|  |  |  |  |
|--|--|--|--|
|  |  |  |  |
|  |  |  |  |
|  |  |  |  |
|  |  |  |  |
|  |  |  |  |
|  |  |  |  |
|  |  |  |  |
|  |  |  |  |
|  |  |  |  |

# Spelling
## Practice Words

| | | | | | |
|---|---|---|---|---|---|
| | | | | | |
| | | | | | |
| | | | | | |
| | | | | | |
| | | | | | |
| | | | | | |
| | | | | | |
| | | | | | |
| | | | | | |

# Spelling
## Practice Words

| | | | | | |
|---|---|---|---|---|---|
| | | | | | |
| | | | | | |
| | | | | | |
| | | | | | |
| | | | | | |
| | | | | | |
| | | | | | |
| | | | | | |
| | | | | | |

@droppinknowledgewithheidi

@droppinknowledgewithheidi

# Spelling

# Spelling

Name:

## Word Building Challenge!

1.
2.
3.
4.
5.
6.
7.
8.
9.
10.

Name:

## Word Building Challenge!

1.
2.
3.
4.
5.
6.
7.
8.
9.
10.

# Spelling

## Word Building Challenge!

Name:

1. _____
2. _____
3. _____
4. _____
5. _____
6. _____
7. _____
8. _____
9. _____
10. _____

# Spelling

## Word Building Challenge!

Name:

1. _____
2. _____
3. _____
4. _____
5. _____
6. _____
7. _____
8. _____
9. _____
10. _____

@droppinknowledgewithheidi

| Short A | Short A |
| --- | --- |
| Practice Word List | Practice Word List |
| hat | hat |
| map | map |
| man | man |
| tab | tab |
| mad | mad |
| bag | bag |
| ram | ram |
| bat | bat |
| lap | lap |
| nab | nab |

# Short A
# Challenge Words

| dab | tap | fan | gab | had |
|-----|-----|-----|-----|-----|
| rag | ham | sap | cat | can |

Say the word. Have the students repeat the word. Then use the word in a sentence & have students spell the word. Remind them to pay attention to the sounds and how we spell them!

**Possible Dictation Sentences:**
Dab: "You need a small dab of glue."
Tap: "I like to tap my fingers to help me spell words."
Fan: "My sister sleeps with a fan on to keep her cool."
Gab: "My grandma has the gift of gab."
Had: "I had a great weekend!"
Rag: "You can use this rag to clean up the mess."
Ham: "Do you like ham on your sandwich?"
Sap: "Maple syrup comes from tree sap."
Cat: "My cat likes to sleep all day."
Can: "We can spell these words."

@droppinknowledgewithheidi

| Short E | Short E |
|---|---|
| Practice Word List | Practice Word List |
| met | met |
| pen | pen |
| bed | bed |
| pet | pet |
| gem | gem |
| hen | hen |
| jet | jet |
| vet | vet |
| wed | wed |
| Ken | Ken |

@droppinknowledgewithheidi  @droppinknowledgewithheidi

# Short E
# Challenge Words

| set | Jen | red | wet | web |
|-----|-----|-----|-----|-----|
| let | men | net | get | yes |

Say the word. Have the students repeat the word. Then use the word in a sentence & have students spell the word. Remind them to pay attention to the sounds and how we spell them!

## Possible Dictation Sentences:
Set: "Please set your plate on the table."
Jen: "I like to play with Jen at recess."
Red: "A stop sign is red."
Wet: "My shoes got wet when I jumped in a puddle."
Web: "The spider made a web by my door."
Let: "My sister let me play with her toy."
Men: "The men are working on the roof."
Net: "Can you catch a butterfly with this net?"
Get: "Let's get some ice cream tonight!"
Yes: "Can you write this word? YES, I can!"

@droppinknowledgewithheidi

| Short I | Short I |
|---|---|
| Practice Word List | Practice Word List |
| pin | pin |
| hit | hit |
| big | big |
| sip | sip |
| lid | lid |
| rip | rip |
| bit | bit |
| win | win |
| zip | zip |
| tin | tin |

@droppinknowledgewithheidi @droppinknowledgewithheidi

# Short I
## Challenge Words

| pig | fin | bin | dig | kid |
|-----|-----|-----|-----|-----|
| tip | did | him | dip | kit |

Say the word. Have the students repeat the word. Then use the word in a sentence & have students spell the word. Remind them to pay attention to the sounds and how we spell them!

**Possible Dictation Sentences:**
Pig: "The pig rolled in the mud."
Fin: "I can see the shark's fin."
Bin: "Put the can in the recycle bin."
Dig: "The dog can dig."
Kid: "We have a new kid in our class."
Tip: "I have a tip for you."
Did: "Did you have a good week?"
Him: "I helped him with his work."
Dip: "I like to dip my chips in queso."
Kit: "We keep a first aid kit in our car."

@droppinknowledgewithheidi

| Short O | Short O |
|---|---|
| Practice Word List | Practice Word List |
| cod | cod |
| pop | pop |
| sob | sob |
| cob | cob |
| rot | rot |
| pom | pom |
| cot | cot |
| mop | mop |
| got | got |
| bop | bop |

# Short O
# Challenge Words

| not | mop | pot | hot | jot |
|-----|-----|-----|-----|-----|
| mom | fox | top | box | rod |

Say the word. Have the students repeat the word. Then use the word in a sentence & have students spell the word. Remind them to pay attention to the sounds and how we spell them!

## Possible Dictation Sentences:
Not: "Do not forget to brush your teeth."
Mop: "We mop the floor on Saturday."
Pot: "Put the carrots in the pot."
Hot: "It is hot in the summer."
Jot: "I will jot down some notes."
Mom: "I will ask my mom if we can have a snack."
Fox: "The fox ran fast."
Top: "Can you climb to the top?"
Box: "What is in the box?"
Rod: "I will get my fishing rod."

@droppinknowledgewithheidi

| Short U | Short U |
|---|---|
| ## Practice Word List | ## Practice Word List |
| hut | hut |
| bud | bud |
| nun | nun |
| rug | rug |
| cub | cub |
| mut | mut |
| fun | fun |
| sub | sub |
| nut | nut |
| bun | bun |

@droppinknowledgewithheidi @droppinknowledgewithheidi

# Short U
# Challenge Words

| bus | cup | cut | gum | mud |
|-----|-----|-----|-----|-----|
| mug | run | but | tub | pup |

Say the word. Have the students repeat the word. Then use the word in a sentence & have students spell the word. Remind them to pay attention to the sounds and how we spell them!

**Possible Dictation Sentences:**
Bus: "Hurry up so you do not miss the bus!"
Cup: "I have a cup of water."
Cut: "Please cut carefully on the line."
Gum: "Would you like a piece of gum?"
Mud: "I like to make mud pies after it rains."
Mug: "My teacher drinks coffee from a mug."
Run: "I can run super fast."
But: "I want to play, but I have to clean my room first."
Tub: "I take a bath in the tub."
Pup: "I got my dog when she was just a pup!"

@droppinknowledgewithheidi

| Long Vowels | Long Vowels |
|---|---|
| Practice Word List | Practice Word List |
| go | go |
| so | so |
| me | me |
| he | he |
| I | I |

@droppinknowledgewithheidi

@droppinknowledgewithheidi

| Long Vowels | Long Vowels |
|---|---|
| Practice Word List | Practice Word List |
| go | go |
| so | so |
| me | me |
| he | he |
| I | I |

@droppinknowledgewithheidi

@droppinknowledgewithheidi

# Long Vowel
# Challenge Words

| be | we | hi | no | re* |
|----|----|----|----|-----|

Say the word. Have the students repeat the word. Then use the word in a sentence & have students spell the word. Remind them to pay attention to the sounds and how we spell them!

*re is pronounced with the long vowel sound. This gets kids ready for open-syllable long vowels in multisyllabic words such as remember. It is also an introduction to prefixes.

## Possible Dictation Sentences:
Be: "Will you be at the party on Friday?"

We: "We like to go to the park."

Hi: "Hi Ken! How are you today?"

No: "No, we cannot go to the party."

Re: "Did you **re** – view your work?"

| Digraph TH | Digraph TH |
|---|---|
| Practice Word List | Practice Word List |
| with | with |
| math | math |
| thin | thin |
| froth | froth |
| this | this |
| that | that |
| thud | thud |
| cloth | cloth |
| then | then |
| *thab | *thab |

# Digraph TH
# Challenge Words

| moth | them | thump | path | broth |
|------|------|-------|------|-------|
| bath | sloth | than | tenth | *thig |

Say the word.  Have the students repeat the word. Then use the word in a sentence & have students spell the word. Remind them to pay attention to the sounds and how we spell them!

**Possible Dictation Sentences:**
Moth: "The moth flew away."
Them: "I will play with them on the playground."
Thump: "The dog landed with a thump."
Path: "Follow the path to the party."
Broth: "The broth in the soup was tasty."
Bath: "I got in the bath last night."
Sloth: "The sloth ate a banana."
Than: "The dog is taller than me." *clearly state the /a/ and listen carefully when they repeat it.*
Tenth: "I came in tenth place."
Thig: "Thig is a nonsense word."

| Digraph SH | Digraph SH |
| --- | --- |
| Practice Word List | Practice Word List |
| fish | fish |
| ship | ship |
| sham | sham |
| brush | brush |
| dish | dish |
| cash | cash |
| smash | smash |
| crush | crush |
| shin | shin |
| *tesh | *tesh |

# Digraph SH
# Challenge Words

| wish | shop | stash | shut | crash |
|------|------|-------|------|-------|
| shim | mesh | rush | gash | *smish |

Say the word. Have the students repeat the word. Then use the word in a sentence & have students spell the word. Remind them to pay attention to the sounds and how we spell them!

**Possible Dictation Sentences:**
Wish: "I wish the sun would come out."
Shop: "When will the shop open?"
Stash: "I keep my candy stash in the drawer."
Shut: "She shut the top before the snake got out."
Crash: "The large crash scared the baby."
Shim: "He used a shim to level the floor."
Mesh: "The mesh screen keeps the bugs outside."
Rush: "Do not rush through the job."
Gash: "The gash on her head is bleeding."
Smish: "Smish is a nonsense word."

@droppinknowledgewithheidi

| Digraph WH/PH | Digraph WH/PH |
|---|---|
| Practice Word List | Practice Word List |
| whisk | whisk |
| graph | graph |
| aphid | aphid |
| which | which |
| whiz | whiz |
| *pham | *pham |
| *whab | *whab |
| *whud | *whud |
| *phim | *phim |
| *whep | *whep |

@droppinknowledgewithheidi
@droppinknowledgewithheidi

# Digraph WH/PH
# Challenge Words

| whip | graphs | when | whim | photo |
|------|--------|------|------|-------|
| *whob | *phep | *whesh | *phum | *whad |

Say the word.  Have the students repeat the word. Then use the word in a sentence & have students spell the word. Remind them to pay attention to the sounds and how we spell them!

**Possible Dictation Sentences:**
Whip: "The whip was by the rider's side."
Graphs: "The graphs help me understand."
When: "When will you be home?"
Whim: "They left on a whim, quickly without a thought."
Phonics: "Phonics helps us hear sounds."
The rest are nonsense words using WH to spell /wh/ and PH to spell /f/— POINT THIS OUT TO THE KIDS: ***whob, phep, whesh, phum, whad

@droppinknowledgewithheidi

| Digraph CH | Digraph CH |
|---|---|
| Practice Word List | Practice Word List |
| chip | chip |
| rich | rich |
| inch | inch |
| chat | chat |
| chomp | chomp |
| munch | munch |
| champ | champ |
| ranch | ranch |
| chug | chug |
| *ched | *ched |

# Digraph CH
# Challenge Words

| munch | chin | bunch | chimp | chop |
|-------|------|-------|-------|------|
| bench | chap | lunch | chest | *chom |

Say the word. Have the students repeat the word. Then use the word in a sentence & have students spell the word. Remind them to pay attention to the sounds and how we spell them!

**Possible Dictation Sentences:**
Munch: "I munch on the crackers for lunch."
Chin: "Touch your finger to your chin."
Bunch: "Put the socks in a bunch."
Chimp: "Why does the chimp eat bananas?"
Chop: "They will chop the celery."
Bench: "I left my drink on the bench."
Chap: "The chap did not like to sleep, he wanted to play."
Lunch: "What will we eat for lunch?"
Chest: "Mom rubbed my chest."
Chom: "Chom is a nonsense word."

| Digraph NG | Digraph NG |
|---|---|
| Practice Word List | Practice Word List |
| going | going |
| bring | bring |
| song | song |
| ding | ding |
| hang | hang |
| king | king |
| swing | swing |
| thing | thing |
| stung | stung |
| *lang | *lang |

@droppinknowledgewithheidi @droppinknowledgewithheidi

# Digraph NG
# Challenge Words

| long | sing | bang | ring | fang |
|------|------|------|------|------|
| wing | cling | sting | lung | *shung |

Say the word. Have the students repeat the word. Then use the word in a sentence & have students spell the word. Remind them to pay attention to the sounds and how we spell them!

**Possible Dictation Sentences:**
Long: "The hair was long on the cat."
Sing: "Can you sing the words?"
Bang: "He will bang on the pot with a spoon."
Ring: "They lost the ring."
Fang: "The fang on the tiger was sharp."
Wing: "The wing on the butterfly was red."
Cling: "Don't cling to the walls, run around."
Sting: "The burn will sting."
Lung: "The cow's lung was big."
Shung: "Shung is a nonsense word."

| Floss Rule | Floss Rule |
|---|---|
| Practice Word List | Practice Word List |
| will | will |
| shall | shall |
| toss | toss |
| huff | huff |
| floss | floss |
| snuff | snuff |
| still | still |
| mess | mess |
| chess | chess |
| *fass | *fass |

@droppinknowledgewithheidi  @droppinknowledgewithheidi

# Floss Rule
# Challenge Words

| well | drill | tell | boss | puff |
|------|-------|------|------|------|
| pass | loss | hill | bluff | *snill |

Say the word. Have the students repeat the word. Then use the word in a sentence & have students spell the word. Remind them to pay attention to the sounds and how we spell them!

**Possible Dictation Sentences:**
Well: "I dropped the rock in the well."
Drill: "The drill was broken and they bought a new one."
Tell: "When will you tell the funny story?"
Boss: "We lost our boss and had to find her."
Puff: "A puff of smoke blew away from the campfire."
Pass: "Please pass the potatoes."
Loss: "After the loss, the team had a meeting."
Hill: "She made it up the hill, but was tired."
Bluff: "The side of the bluff was steep."
Snill: "Snill is a nonsense word."

| S Blends | S Blends |
| --- | --- |
| Practice Word List | Practice Word List |
| still | still |
| sloth | sloth |
| snap | snap |
| step | step |
| spin | spin |
| stamp | stamp |
| stem | stem |
| swim | swim |
| sled | sled |
| skip | skip |

@droppinknowledgewithheidi  @droppinknowledgewithheidi

# Beginning S-Blends
# Challenge Words

| skin | stomp | smash | slim | swish |
|------|-------|-------|------|-------|
| slam | spot | skill | swing | slot |

Say the word. Have the students repeat the word. Then use the word in a sentence & have students spell the word. Remind them to pay attention to the sounds and how we spell them!

## Possible Dictation Sentences:
Skin: "His skin is soft."
Stomp: "Please do not stomp on the way to lunch."
Smash: "We can smash this dish."
Slim: "She is tall and slim."
Swish: "I can swish the basketball into the net."
Slam: "The door will slam shut."
Spot: "The dog has a brown spot on his eye."
Skill: "I can learn a new skill."
Swing: "She likes to swing but I like the slide."
Slot: "Drop the token in the slot."

@droppinknowledgewithheidi

| L Blends | L Blends |
|---|---|
| Practice Word List | Practice Word List |
| plug | plug |
| cliff | cliff |
| club | club |
| flash | flash |
| flip | flip |
| floss | floss |
| glass | glass |
| blimp | blimp |
| plot | plot |
| clam | clam |

# Beginning L-Blends
# Challenge Words

| clap | flag | clip | flat | glad |
|------|------|------|------|------|
| plant | plum | blend | class | flop |

Say the word. Have the students repeat the word. Then use the word in a sentence & have students spell the word. Remind them to pay attention to the sounds and how we spell them!

**Possible Dictation Sentences:**
Clap: "Please clap for the performance."
Flag: "The red flag means stop."
Clip: "Can you clip the papers together?"
Flat: "My mom got a flat tire."
Glad: "I am so glad you are here!"
Plant: "Can you help me plant this flower?"
Plum: "I had a plum for lunch."
Blend: "G-L is a blend."
Class: "Our class is the best!"
Flop: "That movie was a flop."

@droppinknowledgewithheidi

| R Blends | R Blends |
| --- | --- |
| Practice Word List | Practice Word List |
| crab | crab |
| drip | drip |
| drum | drum |
| frost | frost |
| grass | grass |
| print | print |
| trim | trim |
| branch | branch |
| grub | grub |
| brim | brim |

# Beginning R-Blends
# Challenge Words

| brush | crash | drop | frog | grab |
|-------|-------|------|------|------|
| grin | trap | grill | crunch | grip |

Say the word. Have the students repeat the word. Then use the word in a sentence & have students spell the word. Remind them to pay attention to the sounds and how we spell them!

**Possible Dictation Sentences:**
Brush: "I like to brush my hair at night."
Crash: "Do not crash into that tree."
Drop: "I will drop you off at nine."
Frog: "The green frog caught a fly."
Grab: "Can you grab my keys, please?"
Grin: "I grin when I am happy."
Trap: "He set up a trap."
Grill: "My dad loves to cook on the grill in the summer."
Crunch: "The leaves crunch as a I walk on them."
Grip: "She has a tight grip."

| Blend NK | Blend NK |
|---|---|
| Practice Word List | Practice Word List |
| thank | thank |
| wink | wink |
| blink | blink |
| drank | drank |
| tank | tank |
| skunk | skunk |
| bank | bank |
| pink | pink |
| shrink | shrink |
| *thunk | *thunk |

# Ending Blend NK
# Challenge Words

| drink | thank | rink | sink | link |
|-------|-------|------|------|------|
| rank | sank | sunk | chunk | *blonk |

Say the word.  Have the students repeat the word. Then use the word in a sentence & have students spell the word. Remind them to pay attention to the sounds and how we spell them!

## Possible Dictation Sentences:
Drink: "I will drink all of the water."
Thank: "I will write a thank you note."
Rink: "When will the ice rink open?"
Sink: "Use the sink to wash your dishes."
Link: "The link did not work on my iPad."
Rank: "Did you rank your favorite candy?"
Sank: "The money sank to the bottom of the pool."
Sunk: "The heavy rock sunk into the wet sand."
Chunk: "I took a large chunk of wood."
Blonk: "Blonk is a nonsense word."

| Digraph CK | Digraph CK |
| --- | --- |
| Practice Word List | Practice Word List |
| black | black |
| pick | pick |
| pack | pack |
| back | back |
| sick | sick |
| sock | sock |
| tick | tick |
| stack | stack |
| duck | duck |
| *thock | *thock |

# Ending Digraph CK
# Challenge Words

| sack | pluck | lock | stick | rock |
|------|-------|------|-------|------|
| shock | block | luck | chick | *zick |

Say the word. Have the students repeat the word. Then use the word in a sentence & have students spell the word. Remind them to pay attention to the sounds and how we spell them!

**Possible Dictation Sentences:**
Sack: "They had everything for the day in the sack."
Pluck: "The chicken has feathers to pluck."
Lock: "I forgot to lock the door."
Stick: "Where did the dog hide the stick?"
Rock: "How big is your rock collection?"
Shock: "Will the metal shock you?"
Block: "I will carry the block to your big tower."
Luck: "The luck ran out and we lost the game."
Chick: "The baby chick ate the seed off the ground."
Zick: "Zick is a nonsense word."

@droppinknowledgewithheidi

| -ED Ending | -ED Ending |
|---|---|
| Practice Word List | Practice Word List |
| landed | landed |
| pushed | pushed |
| asked | asked |
| kicked | kicked |
| dressed | dressed |
| brushed | brushed |
| punched | punched |
| ended | ended |
| crushed | crushed |
| spilled | spilled |

# -ED Ending
# Challenge Words

| jumped | checked | thanked | missed | rushed |
| --- | --- | --- | --- | --- |
| fixed | locked | fluffed | handed | mixed |

Say the word.  Have the students repeat the word. Then use the word in a sentence & have students spell the word. Remind them to pay attention to the sounds and how we spell them!

## Possible Dictation Sentences:
Jumped: "He jumped over the puddle."
Checked: "She checked her word twice."
Thanked: "I thanked Mrs. Smith for the card."
Missed: "We missed you when you were gone!"
Rushed: "We rushed to the dentist because we were late."
Fixed: "He fixed the flat tire."
Locked: "My mom locked the door when she left."
Fluffed: "Dad fluffed my pillow for me."
Handed: "She handed me a letter."
Mixed: "We mixed the batter for the cake."

@droppinknowledgewithheidi

| S as /z/ | S as /z/ |
|---|---|
| Practice Word List | Practice Word List |
| has | has |
| is | is |
| tells | tells |
| hugs | hugs |
| visit | visit |
| pens | pens |
| kids | kids |
| malls | malls |
| yams | yams |
| *luns | *luns |

@droppinknowledgewithheidi  @droppinknowledgewithheidi

# S as /z/
## Challenge Words

| as | his | bugs | runs | jams |
|------|-------|-------|------|-------|
| tans | calls | bells | hens | *fens |

Say the word. Have the students repeat the word. Then use the word in a sentence & have students spell the word. Remind them to pay attention to the sounds and how we spell them!

## Possible Dictation Sentences:
As: "She will walk as she counts."
His: "That was his dog."
Bugs: "There were so many bugs outside."
Runs: "She runs very fast."
Jams: "Mr. Meyer always jams the copier."
Tans: "The cat tans in the sun."
Calls "The principal calls out my name."
Bells: "Do you know where the bells are?"
Hens: "The hens made a lot of noise this morning."
Fens: "Fens is a nonsense word."

@droppinknowledgewithheidi

| VCe | VCe |
|---|---|
| Practice Word List | Practice Word List |
| use | use |
| came | came |
| make | make |
| gave | gave |
| like | like |
| time | time |
| here | here |
| those | those |
| have | have |
| *sibe | *sibe |

@droppinknowledgewithheidi @droppinknowledgewithheidi

# Teacher Directions

## VCe
## Challenge Words

| ate | made | take | five | ride |
|------|------|------|------|------|
| white | these | live | give | *bape |

Say the word. Have the students repeat the word. Then use the word in a sentence & have students spell the word. Remind them to pay attention to the sounds and how we spell them!

**Possible Dictation Sentences:**
Ate: "They ate a good meal."
Made: "He made a beautiful picture."
Take: "What will you take to the zoo?"
Five: "There are five fish in the water."
Ride: "The ride at the park was full."
White: "The white paper was gone."
These: "These are my favorite students."
Live: "The show was taped live and we were there."
Give: "Did you give them a compliment?"
Bape: "Bape is a nonsense word."

| Soft C | Soft C |
|---|---|
| Practice Word List | Practice Word List |
| cent | cent |
| race | race |
| nice | nice |
| face | face |
| rice | rice |
| lace | lace |
| ice | ice |
| cell | cell |
| decent | decent |
| twice | twice |

# Soft C
# Challenge Words

| dance | spice | recent | mice | trace |
|-------|-------|--------|------|-------|
| slice | space | price | fence | pace |

Say the word. Have the students repeat the word. Then use the word in a sentence & have students spell the word. Remind them to pay attention to the sounds and how we spell them!

**Possible Dictation Sentences:**
Dance: "Do you like to dance?"
Spice: "We need to add some pumpkin pie spice."
Recent: "Did you see the most recent update?"
Mice: "There are mice in the attic."
Trace: "Trace this word with your marker."
Slice: "I would like a slice of pizza, please."
Space: "Make sure you put a space in between words."
Price: "The price is too high."
Fence: "We are going to paint the fence white."
Pace: "Can you pick up the pace?"

| Soft G | Soft G |
|---|---|
| Practice Word List | Practice Word List |
| gem | gem |
| huge | huge |
| gist | gist |
| sage | sage |
| cage | cage |

| Soft G | Soft G |
|---|---|
| Practice Word List | Practice Word List |
| gem | gem |
| huge | huge |
| gist | gist |
| sage | sage |
| cage | cage |

# Soft G
## Challenge Words

| age | magic | page | rage | wage |
|-----|-------|------|------|------|

Say the word. Have the students repeat the word. Then use the word in a sentence & have students spell the word. Remind them to pay attention to the sounds and how we spell them!

**Possible Dictation Sentences:**

Age: "What is your age?"

Magic: "Let me show you this cool magic trick."

Page: "What page are we on?"

Rage: "He was shaking with rage."

Wage: "She earns a weekly wage."

| Vowel Team EE | Vowel Team EE |
|---|---|
| ## Practice Word List | ## Practice Word List |
| see | see |
| green | green |
| peel | peel |
| queen | queen |
| jeep | jeep |
| feet | feet |
| seed | seed |
| meet | meet |
| weep | weep |
| *shreen | *shreen |

@droppinknowledgewithheidi  @droppinknowledgewithheidi

# Teacher Directions

## Vowel Team EE
## Challenge Words

| keep | sleep | heel | teeth | wheel |
|------|-------|------|-------|-------|
| weed | sleet | three | peels | *zeel |

Say the word.  Have the students repeat the word. Then use the word in a sentence & have students spell the word. Remind them to pay attention to the sounds and how we spell them!

**Possible Dictation Sentences:**
Keep: "Will you keep the rabbit?"
Sleep: "I go to sleep at 8 p.m."
Heel: "The heel of her foot was hurt."
Teeth: "I haven't lost any teeth."
Wheel: The wheel of the bike was broken."
Weed: The weed was tall and hard to pull."
Sleet: "Last night, the sleet fell from the sky."
Three: "The three pigs were safe from the wolf."
Peels: "The dog ate all the apple peels."
Zeel: "Zeel is a nonsense word."

| Vowel Team EA | Vowel Team EA |
|---|---|
| Practice Word List | Practice Word List |
| eat | eat |
| clean | clean |
| beach | beach |
| lead | lead |
| seal | seal |
| beans | beans |
| tea | tea |
| leave | leave |
| teach | teach |
| meat | meat |

# Vowel Team EA
# Challenge Words

| sea | read | peach | leaf | clean |
|------|-------|-------|-------|-------|
| team | leash | treat | leads | near |

Say the word. Have the students repeat the word. Then use the word in a sentence & have students spell the word. Remind them to pay attention to the sounds and how we spell them!

## Possible Dictation Sentences:

Sea: "The sea turtles are slow to reach the sand."
Read: "I will read a book to you."
Peach: "The peach tree is very big."
Leaf: "Use the leaf to make a cool art project."
Clean: "He will clean his room and go outside."
Team: "The blue team will be up first."
Leash: "Will the bunny walk on a leash?."
Treat: "They will get a treat after they eat dinner."
Leads: "The band leads the song we sing."
Near: "She was near the chair and sat down."

| Vowel Team AI | Vowel Team AI |
|---|---|
| Practice Word List | Practice Word List |
| stain | stain |
| brain | brain |
| tail | tail |
| rain | rain |
| maid | maid |
| wait | wait |
| bait | bait |
| faint | faint |
| nail | nail |
| pain | pain |

@droppinknowledgewithheidi  @droppinknowledgewithheidi

# Vowel Team AI
# Challenge Words

| train | chain | sail | drain | paid |
|-------|-------|------|-------|------|
| main | paint | plain | braid | laid |

Say the word. Have the students repeat the word. Then use the word in a sentence & have students spell the word. Remind them to pay attention to the sounds and how we spell them!

## Possible Dictation Sentences:

Train: "Alex loved to play with the train set."
Chain: "The chain in the fence was broken."
Sail: "It was hard to sail with no wind."
Drain: "The toy clogged the drain and water filled the sink."
Paid: "They paid a plumber to fix the problem."
Main: "What is the main idea of the story?"
Paint: "We had to paint the room yellow."
Plain: "He eats plain pizza, he doesn't like toppings."
Braid: "The horse has a fancy braid for the show."
Laid: "She laid down and fell asleep quickly."

@droppinknowledgewiththeidi

| Vowel Team AY | Vowel Team AY |
|---|---|
| ## Practice Word List | ## Practice Word List |
| way | way |
| day | day |
| may | may |
| tray | tray |
| stray | stray |
| clay | clay |
| Sunday | Sunday |
| gray | gray |
| spay | spay |
| *tay | *tay |

# Vowel Team AY
# Challenge Words

| say | play | hay | ray | spray |
|-----|------|-----|-----|-------|
| stay | bay | lay | jay | *fay |

Say the word. Have the students repeat the word. Then use the word in a sentence & have students spell the word. Remind them to pay attention to the sounds and how we spell them!

## Possible Dictation Sentences:
Say: "They will say the names of their friends."
Play: "The cat will not play with the dog."
Hay: "The hay was for the horse to eat."
Ray: "A small ray of light peeked through the hole."
Spray: "Do not spray the floors with water."
Stay: "I cannot get the dog to stay."
Bay: "She will eat lunch by the bay."
Lay: "I will lay down and rest for a bit."
Jay: "The blue jay flew away when I got close."
Fay: "Fay is a nonsense word."

@droppinknowledgewithheidi

| Vowel Team OA | Vowel Team OA |
| --- | --- |
| Practice Word List | Practice Word List |
| goat | goat |
| coat | coat |
| soap | soap |
| load | load |
| boat | boat |
| unload | unload |
| oak | oak |
| coast | coast |
| throat | throat |
| bloat | bloat |

@droppinknowledgewithheidi    @droppinknowledgewithheidi

## Vowel Team OA
## Challenge Words

| toast | coal | coach | road | float |
|-------|------|-------|------|-------|
| goats | moat | soak | goal | toad |

Say the word. Have the students repeat the word. Then use the word in a sentence & have students spell the word. Remind them to pay attention to the sounds and how we spell them!

### Possible Dictation Sentences:
Toast: "The toast got burnt and no one ate it."
Coal: "The coal in the fire was hot."
Coach: "The coach didn't come to practice."
Road: "What road do I take to get there?"
Float: "Test if the penny will sink or float."
Goats: "We have too many goats."
Moat: "The bridge helped us cross the moat."
Soak: "The rain will soak the clothes hanging outside."
Goal: "They had a goal to be the first to clean the room."
Toad: "The toad made a loud noise."

@droppinknowledgewithheidi

| Vowel Team OW | Vowel Team OW |
| --- | --- |
| ## Practice Word List | ## Practice Word List |
| grown | grown |
| own | own |
| yellow | yellow |
| snow | snow |
| tow | tow |
| elbow | elbow |
| blow | blow |
| slow | slow |
| shadow | shadow |
| crow | crow |

@droppinknowledgewithheidi · @droppinknowledgewithheidi

# Vowel Team OW
# Challenge Words

| show | grow | mow | throw | window |
|------|------|------|-------|--------|
| row | low | stow | flow | blown |

Say the word. Have the students repeat the word. Then use the word in a sentence & have students spell the word. Remind them to pay attention to the sounds and how we spell them!

**Possible Dictation Sentences:**
Show: "Sam will go to the big show."
Grow: "The plant will not grow without water."
Mow: "Will you mow the lawn today?"
Throw: "We will play after we throw away the trash."
Window: "The window was too high to see out."
Row: "Please sit in the first row of desks."
Low: "How low can you go?"
Stow. "If you stow something, you put it somewhere for safe keeping."
Flow: "She watched the water flow down the river."
Blown: "The stick had blown away in the wind."

| Vowel Team IGH | Vowel Team IGH |
| --- | --- |
| ## Practice Word List | ## Practice Word List |
| right | right |
| fight | fight |
| high | high |
| brighter | brighter |
| might | might |
| sunlight | sunlight |
| flight | flight |
| lighting | lighting |
| slight | slight |
| tighten | tighten |

# Vowel Team IGH
# Challenge Words

| light | night | tight | sight | highest |
|-------|-------|-------|-------|---------|
| fright | bright | sigh | thigh | midnight |

Say the word.  Have the students repeat the word. Then use the word in a sentence & have students spell the word. Remind them to pay attention to the sounds and how we spell them!

**Possible Dictation Sentences:**
Light: "Turn the light on."
Night: "The bugs are bad at night."
Tight: "The shoe was tight, so they didn't buy it."
Sight: "She was nowhere in sight."
Highest: "Did you get to the highest level?"
Fright: "Her face was pale with fright."
Bright: "The sun was too bright today."
Sigh: "It is hard not to sigh, when you don't get what you want."
Thigh: "His thigh was bruised after he got hit."
Midnight: "I was asleep at midnight."

@droppinknowledgewithheidi

| L-Controlled | L-Controlled |
|:---:|:---:|
| Practice Word List | Practice Word List |
| fall | fall |
| small | small |
| pull | pull |
| bull | bull |
| always | always |
| alright | alright |
| wall | wall |
| call | call |
| gull | gull |
| wall | wall |

@droppinknowledgewithheidi   @droppinknowledgewithheidi

# L-Controlled Challenge Words

| all | ball | install | tall | stall |
|------|------|---------|------|-------|
| malls | full | hull | dull | also |

Say the word. Have the students repeat the word. Then use the word in a sentence & have students spell the word. Remind them to pay attention to the sounds and how we spell them!

## Possible Dictation Sentences:

All: "I will eat all of the watermelon."
Ball: "The ball was lost in the trees."
Install: "Did they install the app on your phone?"
Tall: "They were not tall enough to ride on the ride."
Stall: "The bathroom stall was very clean."
Malls: "Malls have many stores to shop at."
Full: "The bin was full of Legos."
Hull: "The hull of the ship should be underwater."
Dull: "The sun made the red color dull."
Also: "I will also have cheese on my burger."

| Closed Syllable Exceptions | Closed Syllable Exceptions |
| --- | --- |
| # Practice Word List | # Practice Word List |
| told | told |
| fold | fold |
| cold | cold |
| bold | bold |
| sold | sold |
| mind | mind |
| mild | mild |
| child | child |
| unkind | unkind |
| behind | behind |

@droppinknowledgewithheidi  @droppinknowledgewithheidi

# Closed Syllable Exceptions Challenge Words

| hold | mold | old | find | blind |
|------|------|-----|------|-------|
| kind | gold | wild | retold | unfold |

Say the word.  Have the students repeat the word. Then use the word in a sentence & have students spell the word. Remind them to pay attention to the sounds and how we spell them!

**Possible Dictation Sentences:**
Hold: "Will you please hold my drink?"
Mold: "The mold had to be cleaned."
Old: "I am not old."
Find: "I will find my shoes so we can leave."
Blind: "The blind dog could smell the treat."
Kind: "The hug was from a kind friend."
Gold: "The gold ring was lost."
Wild: "He picked the wild flowers."
Retold: "She retold the funny story."
Unfold: "I will unfold the towel so I can tie-dye it."

@droppinknowledgewithheidi

| Bossy R (ar) | Bossy R (ar) |
|---|---|
| # Practice Word List | # Practice Word List |
| far | far |
| part | part |
| dark | dark |
| star | star |
| shark | shark |
| bark | bark |
| yarn | yarn |
| arm | arm |
| march | march |
| garden | garden |

@droppinknowledgewithheidi          @droppinknowledgewithheidi

# Bossy R (ar)
# Challenge Words

| barn | farm | park | art | start |
|------|------|------|------|--------|
| hard | chart | jar | scarf | market |

Say the word. Have the students repeat the word. Then use the word in a sentence & have students spell the word. Remind them to pay attention to the sounds and how we spell them!

## Possible Dictation Sentences:

Barn: "The barn was red."
Farm: "They went to the farm and met a pig."
Park: "Where is the big park?"
Art: "I went to the art class."
Start: "It is not time for recess to start."
Hard: "The hard math problem took a long time."
Chart: "I use the chart to stay organized."
Jar: "He couldn't get the jar open."
Scarf: "I will wear my scarf because it is cold."
Market: "This little piggy went to the market."

@droppinknowledgewithheidi

| Bossy R (or) | Bossy R (or) |
|---|---|
| Practice Word List | Practice Word List |
| or | or |
| fork | fork |
| corn | corn |
| porch | porch |
| storm | storm |
| sport | sport |
| torch | torch |
| port | port |
| organ | organ |
| born | born |

@droppinknowledgewithheidi  @droppinknowledgewithheidi

# Bossy R (or)
# Challenge Words

| for | form | cord | north | hornet |
|-----|------|------|-------|--------|
| thorn | horn | short | stork | torn |

Say the word. Have the students repeat the word. Then use the word in a sentence & have students spell the word. Remind them to pay attention to the sounds and how we spell them!

**Possible Dictation Sentences:**
For: "I went to the bank for money."
Form: "They will fill out the form before they go."
Cord: "They found a purple cord and made a bracelet."
North: "I went north on the road and got lost."
Hornet: "He was afraid of the hornet."
Thorn: "There was a thorn on the rose."
Horn: "The horn was broken and didn't make noise."
Short: "The short tree was young and needed water."
Stork: "The stork was white."
Torn: "She noticed that her shirt was torn."

@droppinknowledgewithheidi

| Bossy R (er) | Bossy R (er) |
|---|---|
| **Practice Word List** | **Practice Word List** |
| hers | hers |
| after | after |
| number | number |
| faster | faster |
| herd | herd |
| perch | perch |
| fern | fern |
| term | term |
| verb | verb |
| helper | helper |

@droppinknowledgewithheidi

@droppinknowledgewithheidi

# Bossy R (er)
# Challenge Words

| her | under | never | sister | master |
|-----|-------|-------|--------|--------|
| river | perm | winter | jumper | chapter |

Say the word. Have the students repeat the word. Then use the word in a sentence & have students spell the word. Remind them to pay attention to the sounds and how we spell them!

## Possible Dictation Sentences:

Her: "I wanted her to be my friend."
Under: "They went under the bed to hide."
Never: "The cat will never go outside."
Sister: "I want a baby sister."
Master: "She was a master at basketball."
River: "The river was flowing quickly."
Perm: "The perm made their hair curly."
Winter: "The winter weather was too cold for me."
Jumper: "The insect was a jumper and scared me."
Chapter: "What chapter are you reading?"

@droppinknowledgewithheidi

| Bossy R (ir & ur) | Bossy R (ir & ur) |
|---|---|
| ## Practice Word List | ## Practice Word List |
| first | first |
| bird | bird |
| shirt | shirt |
| dirt | dirt |
| birth | birth |
| hurt | hurt |
| blurted | blurted |
| curl | curl |
| fur | fur |
| turn | turn |

# Bossy R (ir & ur)
# Challenge Words

| girl | skirt | chirp | third | birch |
|------|-------|-------|-------|-------|
| burp | curb | turn | church | turnip |

Say the word. Have the students repeat the word. Then use the word in a sentence & have students spell the word. Remind them to pay attention to the sounds and how we spell them!

**Possible Dictation Sentences:**
Girl: "The girl was learning to play chess."
Skirt: "The skirt needed to be cleaned."
Chirp: "The bird will chirp when it is afraid."
Third: "The third place medal was bronze."
Birch: "A birch tree has a special leaf."
Burp: "After you burp say excuse me."
Curb: "I park my bike by the curb."
Turn: "Will you turn around and look at the back?"
Church: "The church building was tall."
Turnip: "The turnip was ready to be eaten."

| Tricky Y (as E) | Tricky Y (as E) |
| --- | --- |
| ## Practice Word List | ## Practice Word List |
| baby | baby |
| sunny | sunny |
| yummy | yummy |
| story | story |
| sleepy | sleepy |
| army | army |
| thirty | thirty |
| dusty | dusty |
| empty | empty |
| filthy | filthy |

# Tricky Y (as E)
# Challenge Words

| funny | candy | bunny | happy | frosty |
|-------|-------|-------|-------|--------|
| gory | muddy | copy | cherry | twenty |

Say the word. Have the students repeat the word. Then use the word in a sentence & have students spell the word. Remind them to pay attention to the sounds and how we spell them!

**Possible Dictation Sentences:**
Funny: "The jokes were funny."
Candy: "The candy was gross."
Bunny: "The bunny was hiding from the dog."
Happy: "What makes you happy?"
Frosty: "The nights in winter are frosty and snow falls."
Gory: "A gory movie is one that has lots of blood."
Muddy: "Take off your muddy shoes."
Copy: "I need a new copy of the page; I messed up."
Cherry: "The cherry fell of the sundae."
Twenty: "All twenty students brought a lunch."

@droppinknowledgewithheidi

| Tricky Y (as I) | Tricky Y (as I) |
|---|---|
| # Practice Word List | # Practice Word List |
| cry | cry |
| fry | fry |
| sly | sly |
| shy | shy |
| apply | apply |
| defy | defy |
| reply | reply |
| July | July |
| my | my |
| ply | ply |

@droppinknowledgewithheidi  @droppinknowledgewithheidi

# Tricky Y (as I)
# Challenge Words

| by | dry | fly | spy | comply |
|------|------|------|------|--------|
| sty | deny | rely | why | myself |

Say the word.  Have the students repeat the word. Then use the word in a sentence & have students spell the word. Remind them to pay attention to the sounds and how we spell them!

**Possible Dictation Sentences:**
By: "I went by your house to see you."
Dry: "Use the towel to dry the dishes, please."
Fly: "The fly was in the house and bothering us."
Spy: "Do not spy on them."
Comply: "When you comply, you do what is asked of you."
Sty: "A pen for pigs is a sty. It can also be an infection in your eye."
Deny: "If they deny you, you can't do something."
Rely: "I rely on you to do what is expected."
Why: "Why are you happy today?"
Myself: "I can tie my shoes by myself."

| Vowel Digraph (long oo) | Vowel Digraph (long oo) |
|---|---|
| **Practice Word List** | **Practice Word List** |
| soon | soon |
| food | food |
| zoom | zoom |
| noon | noon |
| cool | cool |
| boo | boo |
| fool | fool |
| spool | spool |
| root | root |
| scoot | scoot |

# Vowel Digraph (long oo)
# Challenge Words

| moon | pool | spoon | room | tool |
|------|------|-------|------|------|
| zoo | boot | hoot | scoop | stool |

Say the word. Have the students repeat the word. Then use the word in a sentence & have students spell the word. Remind them to pay attention to the sounds and how we spell them!

## Possible Dictation Sentences:
Moon: "The moon is bright tonight."
Pool: "It is so hot; I just want to jump in the pool!"
Spoon: "Use the spoon to eat your ice cream."
Room: "You must clean your room today."
Tool: "A hammer is a helpful tool."
Zoo: "I love going to see the animals at the zoo."
Boot: "He got mud on his boot."
Hoot: "She can hoot like an owl."
Scoop: "I would like one scoop of sherbet please!"
Stool: "He used the stool to reach the cups."

@droppinknowledgewithheidi

## Short OO

### Practice Word List

hook

book

shook

cook

took

## Short OO

### Practice Word List

hook

book

shook

cook

took

## Short OO

### Practice Word List

hook

book

shook

cook

took

## Short OO

### Practice Word List

hook

book

shook

cook

took

# Vowel Digraph (short oo)
# Challenge Words

| look | nook | wood | foot | good |
|------|------|------|------|------|

Say the word. Have the students repeat the word. Then use the word in a sentence & have students spell the word. Remind them to pay attention to the sounds and how we spell them!

**Possible Dictation Sentences:**
Look: "Look at the bird in the tree."

Nook: "I like to read in my book nook."

Wood: "This table is made of wood."

Foot: "I have a sore foot."

Good: "You did a good job today."

| Vowel Digraph (aw) | Vowel Digraph (aw) |
| --- | --- |
| **Practice Word List** | **Practice Word List** |
| drawn | drawn |
| brawl | brawl |
| law | law |
| claw | claw |
| flaw | flaw |
| pawn | pawn |
| thaw | thaw |
| hawk | hawk |
| fawn | fawn |
| squawk | squawk |

@droppinknowledgewithheidi    @droppinknowledgewithheidi

# Vowel Digraph (aw)
# Challenge Words

| saw | draw | raw | lawn | straw |
|------|------|------|------|----------|
| claws | jaw | yawn | paw | withdraw |

Say the word. Have the students repeat the word. Then use the word in a sentence & have students spell the word. Remind them to pay attention to the sounds and how we spell them!

## Possible Dictation Sentences:

Saw: "I saw the movie last night."
Draw: "They will draw a picture with colored pencils."
Raw: "Do not eat the raw food before it is cooked."
Lawn: "Will you mow the lawn before you leave today?"
Straw: "The straw fell out of the cup."
Claws: "The dog had to get his claws clipped."
Jaw: "Relax your jaw to get your back teeth clean."
Yawn: "When you yawn your brain needs oxygen."
Paw: "The cat got a paw stuck in the fence."
Withdraw: "If you withdraw, you are no longer involved."

@droppinknowledgewithheidi

| Diphthong (ow & ou) | Diphthong (ow & ou) |
|---|---|
| **Practice Word List** | **Practice Word List** |
| now | now |
| brown | brown |
| wow | wow |
| plow | plow |
| shower | shower |
| sound | sound |
| cloud | cloud |
| count | count |
| our | our |
| thousand | thousand |

@droppinknowledgewithheidi

# Diphthongs (ow & ou) Challenge Words

| how | down | town | crowd | flower |
|-----|------|------|-------|--------|
| ground | couch | round | found | mouth |

Say the word. Have the students repeat the word. Then use the word in a sentence & have students spell the word. Remind them to pay attention to the sounds and how we spell them!

**Possible Dictation Sentences:**
How: "How will you get to the moon?"
Down: "The puppy could not go down the stairs."
Town: "The town had a big festival with a fair."
Crowd: "The crowd of people were very noisy."
Flower: "I took the flower inside and gave it water."
Ground: "He sat on the ground and looked at the sky."
Couch: "The couch was blue and soft."
Round: "A circle is a round shape."
Found: "They found a large gold coin."
Mouth: "They had too many marshmallows in their mouth."

@droppinknowledgewithheidi

| Diphthong (oi & oy) | Diphthong (oi & oy) |
|:---:|:---:|
| ## Practice Word List | ## Practice Word List |
| join | join |
| foil | foil |
| point | point |
| choice | choice |
| boil | boil |
| toy | toy |
| boy | boy |
| soy | soy |
| enjoy | enjoy |
| loyal | loyal |

# Diphthong (oi & oy)
# Challenge Words

| coin | soil | toilet | spoil | boiling |
|------|------|--------|-------|---------|
| joy | boys | royal | oyster | foyer |

Say the word.  Have the students repeat the word. Then use the word in a sentence & have students spell the word. Remind them to pay attention to the sounds and how we spell them!

**Possible Dictation Sentences:**
Coin: "The coin is brown and worth one cent."
Soil: "I asked them to buy me some soil for the tree."
Toilet: "Did you flush the toilet?"
Spoil: "We have to be quiet so we don't spoil the surprise."
Boiling: "The water is boiling and ready for pasta."
Joy: "A rainbow brings me joy."
Boys: "The boys will sing first."
Royal: "The royal family is about to go on vacation."
Oyster: "He found an oyster shell on the beach."
Foyer: "A foyer is an open area at the entrance of a building."

@droppinknowledgewithheidi

| Schwa | Schwa |
| --- | --- |
| Practice Word List | Practice Word List |
| banana | banana |
| zebra | zebra |
| camel | camel |
| lemon | lemon |
| tomorrow | tomorrow |
| dinosaur | dinosaur |
| basket | basket |
| father | father |
| blanket | blanket |
| dragon | dragon |

@droppinknowledgewithheidi · @droppinknowledgewithheidi

# Schwa
# Challenge Words

| salad | pencil | bacon | carrot | jacket |
|---|---|---|---|---|
| helmet | nickel | hundred | gallon | cotton |

Say the word. Have the students repeat the word. Then use the word in a sentence & have students spell the word. Remind them to pay attention to the sounds and how we spell them!

**Possible Dictation Sentences:**
Salad: "I will have a salad for lunch."
Pencil: "I need to sharpen my pencil."
Bacon: "He had bacon and eggs for breakfast."
Carrot: "Can you please cut this carrot?"
Jacket: "You will need a jacket because it is chilly."
Helmet: "Make sure you put on your helmet to ride your bike."
Nickel: "Do you have a nickel?"
Hundred: "I have one hundred dollars."
Gallon: "I will buy a gallon of milk."
Cotton: "My shirt is made from cotton."

# Bonus Tips: More Ideas for Practicing Spelling Words

## Connect Graphemes to Phonemes!

What is the spelling pattern you are teaching? What sound does it connect to? Remember the reading brain should be connecting sounds and symbols! A sound wall with graphemes is a great way to support students in spelling. This allows them to see the sound and connect it to a symbol.

Sound walls are a great resource to help our struggling kiddos continue to work with and develop the acquisition of the 44 sounds we have in English. Using sound walls helps us practice **articulation and articulatory gestures** with our students to lock those sounds down in our phonological processor. Get a sound wall here: https://droppinknowledge.com/droppin-knowledge-on-phonics/

## What Is Articulation? What Are Articulatory Gestures?

It is the way we use our mouth, tongue, teeth, vocal box, and air flow in various ways to create the phoneme sounds. Sometimes our students do not understand these features and that contributes to their lack of phonemic awareness and ability to decode words (connect that sound to letter/spelling pattern).

We can teach the basic articulatory features and use mouth pictures as seen above to help give our students control and knowledge of these sounds. The basic features we can teach are as follows:

1.  *Airflow: How* is the airflow working when we create a specific sound. Does the airflow cut off like in the sound /t/? (Place your hand in front of your mouth to feel that quick burst of air.) Does the airflow continue as long as you can until you run out of breath like with the sound /sh/? (Feel the airflow continue on your hand without stopping until you run out of breath.) Or does the airflow go through our nose like with the sound /m/? (Plug your nose and try and say

that sound.) We want to teach kids and bring awareness to where airflow is coming from when they create sounds.

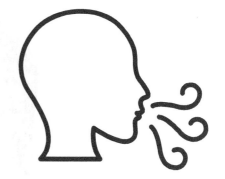

2. *Voicing*: This is talking about, does our voice box shake or vibrate when we create specific sounds? When we introduce sounds we want to teach and bring awareness of this to our students by having them place their fingers on their throats to feel if it vibrates or not. We have sounds that are voiced like /g/ or /v/ and all the vowel sounds. This means that our voice box is activated and vibrates or shakes when we create these sounds. We also have unvoiced sounds that do not shake or activate our voice boxes like /p/ or /ch/.

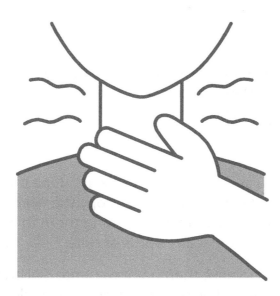

3. *Articulatory or mouth features*: This is teaching the kids what they are doing with their tongue, lips, and teeth when they create different sounds. Are they placing their tongue between their teeth like with the /th/ sound? Are they putting their lips together like in the /p/ sound. Are they pulling their tongue back and creating the sound far in the back of the throat like with the /k/ sound? These mouth movements can be paired and shown with the kid's mouth pictures of a sound wall to help strengthen the kids' understanding of these sounds.

As discussed at the beginning, we want to pair knowledge of these sounds to the grapheme cards (letter or letter pattern) that relate to that specific sound to help our students with their spelling.

## Rainbow Writing

Okay, we know what you are thinking … I've always done that! Us too, but we were doing it the wrong way! We would have kids copy the words and use a different color for each letter. Unless we were just wanting them to work on letter formation, this was not helping them learn words or skills.

A better way to do this is to have them rainbow write SOUNDS! For example, if your spelling word is SHIP, -SH would be one color, -I would be another color, and -P would be another color! This way kids are still working on spelling but aligning this practice to the reading brain!

By making these changes to how you practice and assess spelling, you will see that your kids are much more successful in both reading and writing these words.

# RAINBOW WRITE SOUNDS

# RAINBOW WRITE
# SOUNDS

@droppinknowledgewithheidi

# RAINBOW WRITE SOUNDS

# RAINBOW WRITE SOUNDS

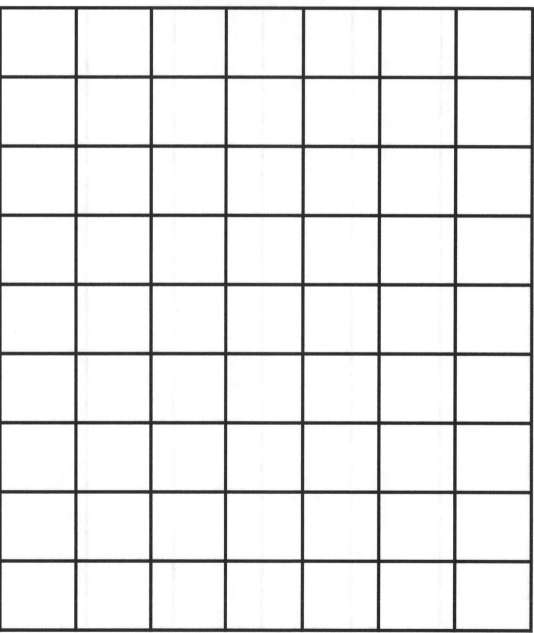

@droppinknowledgewithheidi

# RAINBOW WRITE SOUNDS

@droppinknowledgewithheidi

# RAINBOW WRITE
# SOUNDS

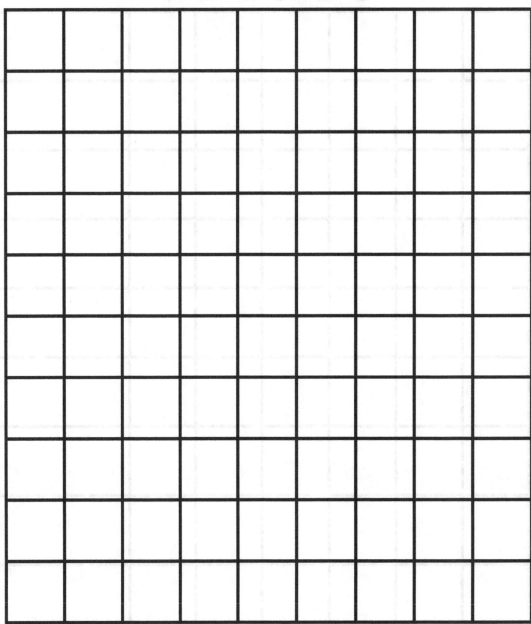

@droppinknowledgewithheidi

# Bonus: Phonics Patterns to Know!

Now that we know we should be teaching phonic skills explicitly and systematically, let's talk about those "rules" that make English seem like it doesn't make any sense!

So first, let's talk about the word "rule." When we call it a rule, it can lead to the assumption that this always happens. However, most phonics patterns have exceptions; therefore, we like to call them patterns instead of rules. Also, as educators or parents, it is easy to get stuck on exceptions to the patterns and we end up missing the big picture. Are there exceptions to the patterns? Yes, there is almost always an exception. But is that where our focus should be? Nope! We are working on trying to establish the kids' understanding of these patterns, because guess what? Usually, the pattern we are teaching is the one they are going to encounter most often. We still can and should talk and teach about exceptions, especially as they come up at various grade levels. But our main priority is to help our kids establish the sound–symbol connection to the pattern that they will encounter most frequently. Then, we can work on teaching the exceptions, so they can build the knowledge around those skills.

**Pro-tip: Exceptions usually have an influence from another language! Etymonline.com is a great resource when you are unsure of why a word is spelled the way it is!**

There are so many phonics patterns that we've learned through our journey, and we are still learning new patterns all the time. We won't list all of those patterns here, but we will share with you a few of our favorites. The patterns we are sharing are those that work enough of the time that we find they are worth teaching!

The following pages will provide an explanation of the phonics or spelling pattern and have activity pages to help you practice or introduce these patterns to your kids.

# What Is the Floss Rule?

The floss rule is that if a word is one syllable with a short vowel, we should double the last letter if it ends with an F, L, S, or Z.

The word "floss" is used because it contains three out of those four letters and follows that pattern.

## Do We Double the Letter When Adding ING ... or Not?

The pattern for adding endings -ING, -EST, -ED, and -ER is typically taught as the 1:1:1 rule. (There is that word rule again!) This states that if a word has one syllable, one vowel, and one consonant, you double the last consonant before adding these endings.

We have also heard this taught as the CVC Rule. If a word or syllable is a CVC word, then you double the last consonant. We do think this makes things more simple for our younger learners.

Our favorite way to teach this is by using a little rhyme that we learned from BrainTrust Tutors.

It goes:

> 1, 2, Double I Do
> 1, 2, 3, No Doubling for Me!

We have included a practice page you can use to practice this with your students.

## Silent E Makes the Vowel Say Its Name ... And Does a Bunch of Other Jobs Too!

When we learned this, it was one of those mind-blowing moments! This explains so many words that we previously thought were spelled irregularly. These patterns are easy to explain to students, as well. They love learning the *why* behind how our words are spelled.

We have included a cheat sheet for silent E patterns for you.

## How Do You Know If You Should Use a C or a K?

This pattern is that in a single-syllable word, we use C if the following vowel is A, O, or U, and we use K if the following vowel is I or E.

Heidi's favorite way to teach this is to draw a cat and a kite using these letters. I first learned this in my training with IMSE, and it is what really helped the pattern stick for me. Then, when I thought back to the pattern, I could picture the drawing!

*Remember this is for words where C makes its hard sound /k/.*

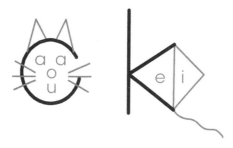

## Is It Park or Parck? How Do We Know When to Use CK?

If you teach kids in the primary grades, we are sure you have seen them spell words like this! How will kids know if it is duck or duk? Clock or clok? Parck or park?

Here is the pattern:

If you hear /k/ at the end of a single syllable word and **that sound immediately follows a short vowel**, it is spelled with a CK.

So, park is spelled with a K because it follows an R-controlled vowel, not a short vowel sound.

You may think that an exception to this pattern is when you see CK in the middle of a word like TICKET. But this is because TICKET is a multisyllabic word, and that first syllable is still following that -CK pattern directly after the short vowel.

## What's Up With the Letter X?

Usually, if we ask a group of people how many sounds there are in the word BOX, most answer 3!

However, X always represents 2 sounds (or phonemes). Sometimes it's the /k/ /s/ sound—as in "box." Other times it's the /g/ /z/ sound—as in "exit."

No matter how you say it, X represents 2 sounds! This is why Louisa Moats calls it a "consonant oddity."

## Quick Tips

- When teaching the letter X, it is best to use target pictures that represent these sounds rather than a picture of a xylophone (where X represents the /z/ sound).

- When mapping words with X, it should take up two boxes or lines since it represents two phonemes!

# G Is for Giraffe & C Is for Circle!

This is one of those patterns that demonstrates why we stopped teaching our students that letters MAKE sounds and started teaching them that letters SPELL or REPRESENT sounds!

G and C typically make their soft sounds (G=/j/ and C=/s/) when followed by E, I, or Y. *Remember, one of the jobs of silent E is to make C and G do this!*

A visual you can use to teach this is called Gentle Cindy. Like the cat/kite pattern we discussed, you draw a face using the letters E, I, and Y and then use G and C on the hair or the earrings. Here is what it might look like!

# How Do You Know When to Use ER, IR, or UR?

Unfortunately, there is no pattern or rule for this. However, there are ways we can teach these spelling patterns to our kids to help them.

We like to teach each pattern separately at first and have kids practice mapping words with that pattern. Since -ER is the most common of these spelling patterns, we usually start there. It also helps to share with my students that -ER is typically used at the end of words.

Remember that with strong foundational skills, mapping a word usually only requires a few repetitions before the word is stored. This is why we find it helpful to spend some time on each pattern and practice through phoneme–grapheme mapping.

Another thing that comes into play with these more difficult spelling patterns is our sight word vocabulary and our brains recognizing patterns. If a student is trying to spell the word "shirt," and if they have had a lot of exposure to that word, and then try to spell it, this sound–symbol connection they have worked on a lot for decoding that word could help them know that the /er/ sound is spelled with -IR and not -UR/-ER. This is the effectiveness of explicit and systematic instruction when working on skills. We are strengthening that orthographic mapping process in the kids' reading brain, so they can use it to their advantage.

## S Spells the Z Sound?

S spells the /z/ sound over 60% of the time! This means that words like IS, HIS, and HAS (which we previously taught to kids to memorize) are perfectly regular and decodable.

There is a pattern for when S represents the /z/ sound. Typically this happens when S follows a voiced sound.

A voiced sound is one that you use your voice box to make. For example, touch your neck and say the sound of the letter B. You should feel a vibration because /b/ is a voiced sound. Now touch your neck again and say the sound of the letter P. You will not feel a vibration for this sound because it is UNvoiced.

In the word BUGS, s represents /z/ because /g/ is a voiced sound.

In the word HATS, s represents /s/ because /t/ is an unvoiced sound.

## ED Makes Three Sounds ... BUT WHY?

For years we taught our first graders that -ED makes three sounds ... /id/ /d/ and /t/. (NOTE: /id/ may be /ed/ depending on dialect.) The kids often asked and wondered why -ED made three sounds. We told them we didn't know because, well, that was the truth!

We have since learned that there is a reason why -ED makes each of its different sounds. It is up to you if you want to teach this to your students or child, but at least now you have an answer if they ask. It can be beneficial to teach for reading and spelling, especially if we see kids decoding and pronouncing -ED endings the wrong way, or if they are spelling -ED with -T, -D, or -ID because that is what they are hearing.

- ED says /id/ or /ed/ when the word ends with a D or a T, and it adds another syllable to the word (e.g. paint—painted).

- ED says /d/ when the word ends with a voiced sound (e.g. play—played).

- ED says /t/ when the word ends with an unvoiced sound (e.g. box—boxed).

## Why Does CH Make All Those Different Sounds?

We typically teach our kids that ch sounds like /ch/ as in cheese or church, right? But then, we come across words like chef, Christmas, and machine! So what's up with that?! Well, it all goes back to etymology, or where the word originated from. CH sounds like /sh/ in words of French origin, and CH sounds like /k/ in words of Greek origin!

## Y as a Vowel

Do you teach your kids that the vowels are A, E, I, O, U, and sometimes Y? Well … Y is actually a vowel more often than a consonant!

Y is a vowel if a word has no other vowels.

Y is a vowel if it comes at the end of a word.

Y is a vowel if it is in the middle of a syllable.

Y is also used in various vowel teams and diphthongs like -AY and -OY.

Y is a consonant when it is the first letter in a word.

Name:

# 3 Sounds of "ED"

If a word ends with a D or a T, adding "ed" will sound like /ed/ or /id/.
If a word ends with a voiced sound, adding "ed" will sound like /d/.
If a word ends with an unvoiced sound, adding "ed" will sound like /t/.

| /id/<br>D or T | /d/<br>voiced sound | /t/<br>unvoiced sound |
|---|---|---|
| landed | moved | crashed |
|  |  |  |
|  |  |  |
|  |  |  |
|  |  |  |
|  |  |  |
|  |  |  |

@droppinknowledge.com

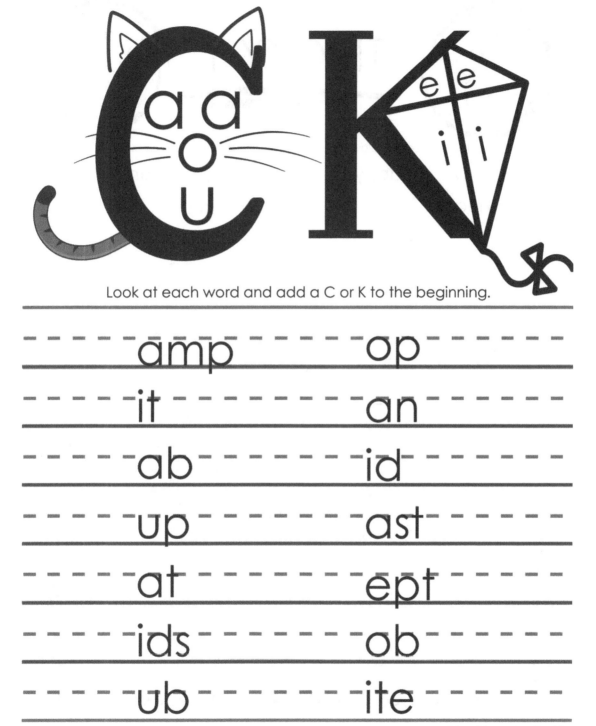

Look at each word and add a C or K to the beginning.

| | |
|---|---|
| amp | op |
| it | an |
| ab | id |
| up | ast |
| at | ept |
| ids | ob |
| ub | ite |

# TRICKY Y

Y as I

Y as E

Read the words below, then write them in the correct column.

| shy | happy | my | cry | funny |
|-----|-------|-----|-----|-------|
| sneaky | tiny | why | cherry | try |

### Y as I

_____

_____

_____

_____

_____

_____

### Y as E

_____

_____

_____

_____

_____

_____

## Read & Draw

It is a <u>sunny</u> day.

I can eat the <u>fry</u>.

# To Double or Not to Double?
## Start counting at the vowel.
Use this when adding vowel suffixes like ed, er, and ing.

hop

land

1, 2 — Double I DO!

1, 2, 3 — NO Doubling for me!

| | |
|---|---|
| ho**pp**ing | landed |
| run | plant |
| big | mash |
| stop | pack |
| web | drink |
| plan | stand |

@droppinknowledgewithheidi

# C and G say their soft sounds when followed by E, I, or Y!

Read each word and highlight the
soft C and/or soft G sound.

| | |
|---|---|
| city | giraffe |
| circle | gym |
| race | gem |
| cent | giant |
| cell | cage |
| germ | nice |

# The Many Jobs of Silent E

Most of us were taught that the job of silent E is to make the vowel say its name, which is true. However, silent E also has about 7 other jobs!

| Makes the vowel Long | Makes sure no words end with an I, V, J, or U |
|---|---|
| vase<br>kite<br>home | glue<br>have |
| **Makes C & G say their soft sounds** | **Makes sure every syllable has a vowel** |
| juice<br>barge | table<br>maple |
| **Shows that a word is not a plural** | **Makes a word look longer** |
| house<br>purse | awe<br>tie |
| **Clarifies meaning** | **Makes TH say its voiced sound** |
| or<br>ore | clothe<br>bathe |

@droppinknowledgewithheidi

# Find all the ER words and write them below.

@droppinknowledgewithheidi

# Find all the IR words and write them below.

# Find all the UR words and write them below.

# Find all the ER words and write them below.

germ

hammer

tiger

# Find all the UR words and write them below.

purse

turn

surf

# Find all the IR words

swirl

bird

skirt

# Bonus Pro-Tips

## What About Students Struggling with Blending?

Have you ever been working with a student and they are looking at a word like MAP. They say the sounds /m/ /a/ /p/ but then when they try to blend the sounds, they say some random word like "football"? Our guess is that you know exactly what we are talking about! Why does this happen?

Well, we happen to think that blending three sound words is actually much harder than we think it is. So here is what we do:

1. *Check phoneme isolation:* If we say the word MAP, can the student isolate and identify the first sound? And we want to make sure they say the sound /m/, not the letter name. If they say the letter name, we say, "Yes, that is the correct letter name, but can you tell me the sound?" It is important that kids know the difference between letters and sounds.
   We also want to check if the student can isolate and identify the ending sound and the middle sound.
   If they cannot quickly do this, they may need more practice with phoneme isolation before they are ready to blend.
2. *Try two sound words first:* If a student can isolate sounds, when you move to blending, start with two sound words—words like "go," "am," "no," "at," "in," etc. This could be a good stepping stone to get ready to blend three sound words. You can use words like "see," "eight," "my," etc. out loud with students to practice blending orally.
3. *Use continuous sounds:* When a child is ready for three sound words, try using words that start with a continuous sound. A continuous sound is one that you can hold for as long as you can hold your breath.
   When you say /s/, you can hold that sound as long as you can. But when you say a sound like /k/, you cannot hold it because it is a stop sound. When kids are blending, using a word like CAT can be a little trickier because it starts with a stop sound. This can make it harder to hear the sounds blending together. Continuous sounds are easier to carry and blend into the next sound, which benefits the kids trying to blend the word.

4. *Try successive blending:* I used to always have kids try to blend with a focus on word families. For example, if the word was HAT, I would try to have them blend /h/ and /at/. This strategy can work for some kids but if they are having trouble with this, successive blending can help!

    With successive blending, if I have a word like HAT, I would actually have the students start with the first sound /h/, then add in the next sound. So they are blending the /h/ and the /a/ first. Now they have /ha/ and then we add in the last sound /t/. We have found this to be helpful with our students who are having trouble. *NOTE: We want to use this as a strategy to help struggling kids with blending, but we want to stop this strategy once students are able to blend more efficiently.*

# Blending with Continuous Sounds

@droppinknowledge.com

| _u_ | _o_ | _i_ | _e_ | _a_ |
|-----|-----|-----|-----|-----|
| fun | rot | sit | set | sat |
| mug | fox | win | fed | map |
| sun | rob | lid | men | rat |
| nut | mop | rip | red | van |
| mud | lot | wig | wet | sap |
| run | not | lip | net | fan |
| rug | fog | fin | leg | mat |

We also want you to know that phonics instruction does not end once the basics have been taught and kids are reading. With our kids who have mastered basic phonics skills and are reading, we can teach morphology, etymology, and advanced phonics skills.

It is also important to focus your explicit and systematic lesson on building and learning each skill in a variety of ways, to help students own that skill.

Here is a general outline of what to teach when you are introducing a new phonics skill.

## Phonemic Awareness

We recommend including phonemic awareness activities at the beginning using the sound connected to that skill. As we discussed earlier with our reading brain, we are learning from speech to print. So, let's get our kids' phonological processor tuned into the sound connected to the skill they will be working on.

## Articulation

After we introduce the new skill, connect it to the articulatory features to reinforce how we create that sound as we are connecting it to that new spelling pattern.

## Application

Next, we need to practice, practice, practice. Work on whole group skills, phoneme–grapheme mapping, practicing words with that skill in isolation, as well as with words in sentences with previously learned skills. You may need some small group practice with those students who we know are not yet understanding, while allowing the others to practice that skill in centers.

## Spelling/Dictation

Then, we want to transfer the practice of working with that skill from decoding (reading) to encoding (spelling), which can be a much more difficult task for students. Students can spell words in isolation with that phonics skill, and then put them into the context of a sentence with previously learned skills.

## Meaning/Vocabulary

Throughout this process we cannot forget about the Simple View of our Reading Brain . . . the meaning processor. We should be talking about the meaning of words that follow our identified phonics skill. This can be done at any (and at multiple) points of the lesson. We should be building vocabulary and background knowledge connected to that skill.

## Connected Text

Finally, we should wrap up our lesson by having our students read decodable books connected to that skill, so they can put that practice into action.

(If you are looking for quality decodable books, we have written our books to be 100% decodable following our scope and sequence. They have been vetted by the Reading League. You can learn more at www.decodableadventureseries.com.)

This format will help solidify the orthographic mapping process of that sound–symbol connection around phonics. We are hitting on a lot of major areas connected to our reading brain with this systematic and explicit approach, which will lead to higher success and our kids locking these skills down!

*If you are looking for lesson plans that follow these steps, we offer done-for-you plans for all phonics skills in our scope & sequence. You can access them inside LitFlix—a subscription for teachers and parents providing resources and training in the Science of Reading. Head to www.scienceofreading101club.com to learn more!*

| Short A | Objective: I can read and spell Short A words | Day 1 25–35 min. |
|---|---|---|
| **Warm Up** | • Isolate beginning sounds.<br>  • I Do: **at, itch**<br>  • We Do: **after, ask, etch**<br>  • You Do: **ice, agitate** | |
| **Introduce letter/sound** | • Show Short A sound card while making /a/ sound/. Make the sound together and focus attention on shape and movement. Your mouth should be half open, tongue inside the bottom of the mouth, the sound is continuous, and the voice box is on/voiced. Practice saying and hearing /a/ at the beginning and middle of words. **(apple, appetizer, at, map, sat, rap, and)**<br>• Remind students how to form the letter a. Start with the c then add line. It is best if this is done without picking up the pencil.<br>• Draw an a if you hear /a/: **ask, jazz, hot, red, hat, hop, fast.** (This can be done in any sensory item—sand, shaving cream, in the air (with their nose, pinky), etc.) | Sound wall, articulation cards, mirrors, sensory item |
| **Practice** | • Practice Short A words using successive blending. First tap each letter saying sound. Then blend the first two sounds together and tap last sound. Blend the word together.<br>  • I Do: **cap, bag, mad**<br>  • We Do: **ran, nap, tab**<br>  • You Do: Finish the pages as needed<br>  • Challenge: nonsense word page<br>• Use slides/ student copy to spell CVC words that have /a/ in them.<br>  • I Do: **map, ham,**<br>  • We Do: **hat, bat, fan, mad, man, cab, nap, rat**<br>  • You Do: **sad, cat, wax, van, dad, tag, jam, can, pad, mat** | Successive Blending Short A<br><br>Tap, Map, Move slides and student copy |
| **Dictation** | • Practice words in isolation for spelling: **hat, map, man, tab**<br>• Introduce the heart word **"the"** with slides. Have students point and say the 2 sounds after it is mapped and then blend them together again. | Whiteboards, Short A word slides (heart word) |
| **Vocabulary** | • Say the word **bat**. Have students draw a picture of what bat means to them. (the animal bat, a bat used in baseball, the action of being at bat)<br>• Have students share what their word means. Add in any definitions students didn't think of. | |
| **Text** | • Use <u>The Jam</u> poem to highlight all of the A-s they find on the page.<br>• Have students say /a/ for each highlight | Decodable poems, highlighter |

@scienceofreading101club.com

| | Objective: | |
|---|---|---|
| **Warm Up** | | |
| **Introduce letter/sound** | | |
| **Practice** | | |
| **Dictation** | | |
| **Vocabulary** | | |
| **Text** | @scienceofreading101club.com | |

# Bonus Phonics Game!

This one is from Heidi and she calls it the Phonics Name Game.

This was an all-time favorite game for my students! I would play this with my first graders during the extra 10–15 minutes we had before lunch. I am not kidding when I tell you that I could not get them to go to lunch! I would have to remind them that they only had a short time to eat and we would play this again tomorrow. When they came back from lunch, they were often still talking about it! So now, you are probably wondering, what is this magical game?

I start with my name as you see in the picture. Then, we dissect it! We talk about the number of syllables first and then get into the different phonics patterns in our names. I want to note right away that there is no right or wrong way to break apart a name. In fact, it will look different depending on the grade you teach!

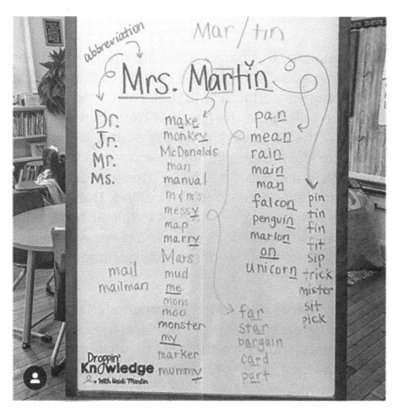

Let's talk about how I did my name with my class.

I started with the abbreviation Mrs. I had not yet explicitly taught abbreviations so we talked about them briefly and my students were still able to come up with some examples.

Then I noted that my last name starts with an M and we said the sound that represents the letter M. I asked my students to come up with more words that started with the /m/ sound. I give my students a chance to talk with a neighbor first and then share out. As they share, I am writing down all the words they are giving me. You will notice I underlined various spelling patterns from the words we wrote down. Some we had learned and talked about and some I was just pointing out to students.

Next in my name is a vowel-R pattern, which we had just learned. So I had my students think of more words with that phonics pattern.

I could have chunked the last part together and had students come up with words that rhyme with TIN but we decided to do short I words and words that end with /n/ instead.

You will notice when you play this game, there are many ways to break up a name. Another fun thing about this game is getting to talk about culture! Most names do not follow phonics patterns (and that's okay)! For example, if I were to use my first name, I can talk about the fact that Heidi comes from the German language so that is why the -EI spells the long /ī/ sound. It is also why my name ends with an -I since we know that no English words end with an -I. When I come across spellings like this, I talk about them but then we focus on the SOUND and finding words with that SOUND, not the spelling. The words your students come up with will give you more opportunities to talk about spelling and phonics patterns naturally! These discussions are also a great way to build background knowledge and help expand other students' oral language vocabulary that may have never heard certain words.

After we completed my name, I would get out anchor chart paper and we would make a phonics poster for each student in my class, throughout the year. Once the poster was complete, I would give students the option to take it home right away or hang it up for a week. (Most of them wanted to hang it up!)

I recommend thinking about how you will break up a name before doing it with the class but don't get stuck on the spellings! Remember, you will talk about the spelling briefly but focus on the sound.

Here are some recommendations by grade level:

**Kindergarten:** You may go letter by letter and just do beginning and ending sounds for each letter in a student's name.

**First Grade:** You may do some letters while also noticing some phonics patterns. Exposure to advanced phonics patterns is okay too!

**Second Grade and Beyond:** You may want to incorporate prefixes, suffixes, advanced phonics, morphology, and etymology patterns as they are available.

Again, remember to have fun and learn along with your students! If you are not sure why a sound is spelled the way it is, it's okay. The phonics name game is a great opportunity to learn more about our students and study phonics and spelling in an authentic way. Head to https://droppinknowledge.com/droppin-knowledge-on-phonics/ to see this in action.

# Wrapping Up

## Ready, Set, Read On! Your Next Steps and Staying in Touch

We hope you found this book to be an easy, practical read with tools that you can use with your child or your students tomorrow. While we covered a lot, I do want to remind you that this is definitely not an all-inclusive book. Our hope is that this gives you a starting point when working with early or struggling readers learning to spell.

If you are a teacher like us who was not explicitly taught how to teach kids to read effectively, remember that you do not know better until you do! The good news is that if we follow what the evidence says, 95% of kids CAN learn to read.

Also remember that while much of what is considered the Science of Reading is established, it is still science and new research is always emerging. We try to attend as many webinars and conferences as we can. We also like to follow the researchers on social media or their websites so we can stay up to date.

We hope you will join Heidi on social media or stay tuned to our website as we continue to share everything we learn and unlearn. Remember, this is a journey! Even well-known researchers and scientists are learning new things all the time.

**If you are looking for more support, resources, and training in the Science of Reading, check out LitFlix! We have created this space to give you the tools and the training you need to teach reading aligned to the research and evidence. We offer over 10,000 pages of resources (and growing) plus access to several training sessions each month. Learn more at www.scienceofreading101club.com.**

Thank you for being open to change and sitting with some uncomfortable feelings as we learn and grow together. Change is not always easy. We often remind ourselves that teaching is not about us, it is about the kids.

We believe that together, we CAN change the literacy statistics!